Cascading Style Sheets:

A Primer

Joseph R. Jones
Paul Thurrott

Cascading Style Sheets:

A Primer

Joseph R. Jones
Paul Thurrott

A division of
Henry Holt and Co., Inc.
New York

MIS:Press
A Division of Henry Holt and Company, Inc.
115 West 18th Street
New York, New York 10011
http://www.mispress.com

Limits of Liability and Disclaimer of Warranty

First Edition—1998

Library of Congress Cataloging-in-Publication Data

```
Jones, Joseph R.
   Cascading Style Sheets / by Joseph R. Jones and Paul Thurrott
      p.      cm.
   ISBN 1-55828-579-2
      1. Thurrott, Paul B.. 2. Title. 3. Web publishing.
I. Thurrott, Paul B. II Title.
   TK5105.888.J653      1997
   005.7'2—dc21                              96-32534
                                                  CIP
```

10 9 8 7 6 5 4 3 2 1

Associate Publisher: *Paul Farrell*

Managing Editor: *Shari Chappell*	**Production Editor:** *Gay Nichols*
Editor: *Debra Williams Cauley*	**Technical Editor:** *Paul Thurrott*
Copy Edit Manager: *Karen Tongish*	**Copy Editor:** *Geneil Breeze*

Contents in Brief

Contents

To Kathy Thomas, to whom I owe much of who and where I am.

-JRJ

To Stephanie

-PBT

ACKNOWLEDGMENTS:

This book would never have had the chance to become a reality were it not for the efforts and patience of a virtual army of people. I could neverthank everyone who played a part, but there are a few that deserve specialmention:

Thanks to Debra Williams-Cauley, Karen Tongish, and the rest of the staff at MIS Press for their patience dealing with the missed deadlines and late submissions so common in book publishing. Thanks also to Adam Ray for neverletting things get boring, and to Paul Thurrott, the Webmaster at Big TentMedia Labs—a good friend who I am lucky enough to work with. Further thanks to the whole staff at Big Tent for dealing with the hours that went into this book instead of other projects. This is the greatest bunch of people I have ever worked with, and I am looking forward to year two! Further thanks to my family for putting up with me for so long, which is no easy task.

I'd also like to thank Sharon Blanton and Dennis Webb for giving me a chance to start a career on the web when there were no careers on the web.

Finally, a special thanks to all the people who played a part in making me what I am. If you're looking to place blame you should talk to James O'Brien, who taught me how to work, Torsten Voss, who taught me what friendship is, Kathy Thomas, who taught me about technology and professionalism, and John Dant, who taught me how to think.

—*Joseph R. Jones*

Introduction

In the beginning there was nothing. Then God said
"Let there be Light!"
There was still nothing, but by God you could see it!

Something similar has occurred in the Web design industry. HTML, originally conceived as a simple mark-up language, has evolved into a complex page layout and multimedia authoring language. "God," this time in the form of Netscape and Microsoft, had given us light, but it is up to us as Web designers to create something worth seeing. Developers quickly realized that filling this void will take much longer than seven days: the industry is awash in competing standards and incompatible methodologies, making deployment of media-rich sites difficult at best, impossible at worst.

This state of affairs prompted the development of this book. With this volume, we hope to arm you, the developer, with the knowledge and tools needed to exploit the new opportunities presented by these new technologies, complete with workarounds for the various incompatibilities created by the differing implementations of such tools as Cascading Style Sheets (CSS) and Dynamic HTML (DHTML). I will assume that you already possess a rudimentary knowledge of HTML.

This book is divided into four parts. Part I explains the evolution of typography and design on the Web, including non-CSS solutions to common design problems. Part II introduces the basics of Cascading Style Sheets. Part III will help you hone your skills by filling out your knowledge with advanced techniques and methods that take advantage of the more esoteric facets of the specification. Finally, Part IV touches on some graphic design theory, explaining in plain English how to use these new technologies to portray information more effectively on the Web.

PART I: TYPOGRAPHY ON THE WEB: THE BEGINNING

Part I begins with in-depth explanations of how designers used HTML in its infancy to approximate the more advanced capabilities made available by CSS. Concepts such as the advanced use of tables and transparent images to control layout are discussed in depth, as are WYSIWYG HTML editors that allow pixel-level control of hypertext layout. Armed with this knowledge, you will be able to ensure that your sites are backward compatible with browsers that predate CSS. There is even a chapter devoted to Microsoft's HTML Layout Control, which allows designers to specify the exact layout of ActiveX controls and HTML elements in ActiveX-compatible browsers.

PART II: WEB DESIGN MATURES: WELCOME TO STYLE SHEETS

Part II introduces basic concepts of the Cascading Style Sheets specification in its various implementations. Included here are tutorials and examples that explain this technology in useful ways, allowing readers to get started right away. The final chapter in Part II explains the ins and outs of planning for and retroactively deploying Cascading Style Sheets in existing Web sites.

PART III: ADVANCED STYLE SHEETS

Part III is your ticket to the bleeding edge. With technologies like Dynamic HTML, JavaScript-enabled StyleSheets, and explanations of how to tailor your site for individual usersí browsers, this part of the book contains most of the fun stuff. With the information in this section, you will become prepared to build Web-based applications that feel more like CD-ROM multimedia titles than ordinary Web pages.

PART IV: GOOD DESIGN: WEB SITES WITH STYLE

No discussion of Cascading Style Sheets would be complete without some explanation of typographical theory and information architecture. Part IV introduces some elementary concepts of design: the tips and tricks that draw the distinction between the big boys of Web design and everyone else. Weíll examine three Web sites that use varying amounts of CSS technology and effective information design to better communicate their message.

CONVENTIONS USED IN THIS BOOK

Throughout this book, I use various conventions to help you understand the information being presented. *Italic type* is used to present new terms to the reader or provide emphasis. HTML or computer code is presented in a **COURIER FONT**. Icons are used to alert you to certain kinds of information.

 Notes contain cross-references to other parts of the book or to other sources of information. They also can contain useful information to supplement the regular text.

Shortcuts can save you time and energy.

The Browser Watch icon highlights differences in the various implementations of certain browsers. When Netscape handles a tag differently than Explorer does, this is where you'll find out.

Warnings are the gems that help you avoid common traps. The lightning-quick product cycle that has become common on the Web has yielded some buggy software. Warnings help you steer clear of these creepy crawlies.

Designer's tips are little tidbits that help you think like a graphic designer. These tips help you communicate information more effectively to your audience and make your site look more professional.

Site Links are references to information contained on the companion Web site, available at http://www.internet-nexus.com/web/design.asp.

USE THE WEB SITE!

As an added bonus, we have created a Web site that includes information and tools that will help you put your newfound knowledge to work. The Web site also includes time-sensitive information that wasn't available when this book was being written. This site will provide up-to-the-minute information about these technologies as they develop. It also will serve as a conduit through which you can communicate directly with us so that we can use your comments to make the next edition of this book that much better.

The site makes extensive use of the technologies introduced in this book, so I hope you will also view it as an example of how to use CSS and Dynamic HTML in practice.

The site, located at http://www.internet-nexus.com/web/design.asp, is also linked to the WinInfo News Database, which includes daily news about the Web industry and developing technologies. This alone makes an occasional visit to the site worthwhile.

TIME TO GET STARTED

Enough talk—we are sure you are ready to get into some of the more juicy technical details of CSS. I hope you find this volume useful. Please take the time to share your comments about the information presented here. My e-mail address is joe@bigtent.com.

Enjoy!

PART I: TYPOGRAPHY ON THE WEB

CHAPTER 1

Basic Typographical Design with HTML

Contrary to popular belief, advanced typography and information design are not impossible to achieve on the Web. Designers armed with the right techniques can still control basic elements of layout with fairly conventional HTML. Before you jump in and start using tools like Cascading Style Sheets, you should see whether you can tackle that design problem with more conventional—and compatible—methods.

INFORMATION DESIGN

Information design is the use of knowledge about the psychology of user interaction with information to communicate more effectively.

For example, when children are first learning to read, they are taught to sound out words a letter at a time, forming syllables, words, and finally whole sentences. As they become more capable readers, this activity ceases and is replaced with a much more efficient methodology.

As advanced readers, we do not read words as collections of individual letters, but instead recognize word shapes and sentence patterns. This is why sentences in ALL CAPS are hard to read: our minds are not used to reading this way, so the word shapes are unfamiliar. When we read sentences printed in capital letters, we are forced to revert to deciphering individual letters. Because we are more experienced readers, we don't even realize that we are doing it; we simply notice it is taking longer to read a passage. Similarly, we use the layout of information to better understand the flow of content. As designers, we can use this tendency to our advantage in communicating our message. For example, you will notice that the left margin on this page is much wider than the right. This helps give our eyes an opportunity to "catch" the first letter of each line as they move down the page. You will also notice that the various levels of headings have narrower margins, creating an informational hierarchy similar to an outline. This is effective use of white space.

As designers, we do not look at layouts in terms of elements on a sheet of paper or computer screen. Rather we consider the visual hierarchy of elements and their surrounding white space. White space can be the margins on a page, the indentations of paragraphs, or the visual break between elements. In short, white space is the absence of graphical or typographical elements. The effective use of white space is the cornerstone of effective information design.

A full explanation of the finer points of information design is beyond the scope of this book. I recommend picking up *On Stone: The Art and Use of Typography on the Personal Computer*, which focuses on typography in interactive design. For more information on this book and for a list of information design resources, go to http://www.internet-nexus.com/web/design.asp.

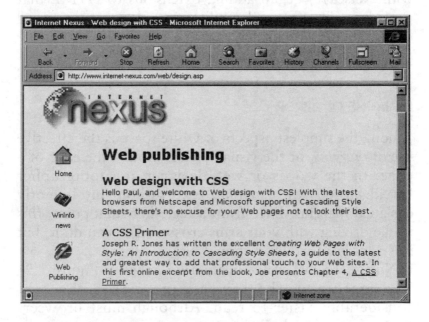

Figure 1.1 The Internet Nexus site includes a list of information design resources.

Unfortunately, the first Web browsers and sites were created by computer programmers and enthusiasts rather than graphic designers. Components of information design were not priorities, so no control over white space or advanced page layout was included in the initial implementations. The developers who were creating Web pages soon started collaborating with graphic designers, who were shocked at the lack of typographical control available in HTML. In time, workarounds were developed that allowed more control, and the companies creating browser software (starting with Netscape) began adding extensions to HTML that provided even greater flexibility. As a designer, you need to understand how to leverage these extensions to create more effective Web pages.

MARGINS OF ERROR

Among the simplest aspects of white space is the effective use of *margins*, or the visual gutters around the edge of a page. In the words of web designer and fontgrapher David Siegel, you can read text without intelligently designed margins, but "from a legibility standpoint, this is like driving with your arms crossed. You can do it, but it is a lot harder than it should be."

Notice the difference in the two pages in Figure 1.2? The margin in the lower page makes the text considerably easier to read. Although most browsers do not provide a built-in construct for management of margins, the effect is easy to approximate using tables.

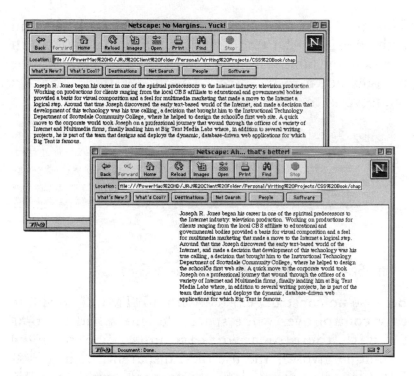

Figure 1.2 *Margins make text easier to read. This margin was created with a simple HTML table.*

The code to produce this effect is really quite simple:

```
<TABLE BORDER=0>
    <TR><TD WIDTH="150"> </TD>
    <TD WIDTH="350">
        This is where the content goes...
    </TD></TR>
</TABLE>
```

This gives you fairly good control over both left and right margins. Through manipulation of the **WIDTH** values in the table cells, you can tweak the width of your margins down to the pixel. Admittedly, this is a hack, but it works in most browsers.

 Microsoft's Internet Explorer introduced margin control to the Web. Included in the BODY tag, the TOPMARGIN and LEFTMARDGIN arguments allow for precise control over page margins. However, this feature is not yet widely supported, so make sure that sites dependent on Explorer's margin controls are viewed and tested in some older browsers to make sure layout is acceptable.

WHITE SPACE CONTROL WITH TRANSPARENT GIFS

Because no construct existed within HTML to facilitate easy control over white space, designers had to come up with their own workarounds. The primary technique involves the use of transparent, or invisible, GIF files to position elements precisely within a page. For example, let's say that you want to indent the first character of a paragraph. HTML provides no **<INDENT>** tag, so you will have to place a transparent GIF before the first letter, and size it appropriately, as shown in Figure 1.3.

```
<IMG SRC="./images/pixel.gif" HEIGHT="1" WIDTH="12"
ALT=" ">
This would be the paragraph.
<P>
```

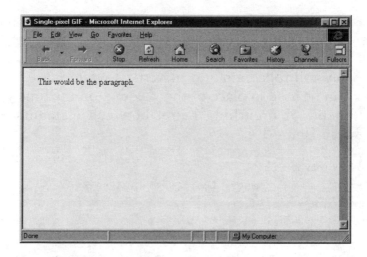

Figure 1.3 A single-pixel GIF lets you precisely position other elements.

This image, now sized with the **WIDTH** argument to be exactly 12 pixels wide, will push the text out of its way and provide the indention that you are seeking. The image will be invisible, assuming that you have handled the transparency correctly, and the file size is not only negligible because it is only one color and one pixel but also because it will be cached—users will need to load this file only once.

Be careful using transparent GIF files on complex pages. Certain browsers (Including Netscape 2.X for Windows 95) will eliminate transparency when memory gets low. As a result, your transparent images will either revert to "Netscape Gray" or to your background color. (The background color may not seem to be a problem until you consider pages that use an image as a background.) Low memory situations occur frequently in pages that have complex nested tables or frames.

Transparent GIFs can also be used for vertical positioning. When followed by a **
** tag, these images will push the content that follows them down, providing an easily controlled amount of vertical white space. This trick can be used in place of the **<P>** tag, or any time you need a bit of breathing room between elements, as shown in Figure 1.4.

```
This is paragraph 1.
<BR><IMG SRC="./images/pixel.gif" HEIGHT="12"
WIDTH="1"><BR>
This is paragraph 2.
```

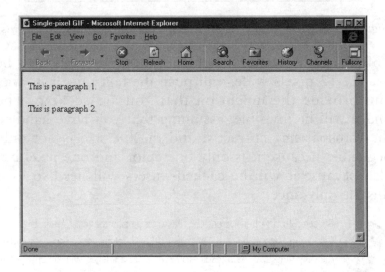

Figure 1.4 *Transparent GIFs can also be used for vertical positions.*

In this example, we are again using 12 pixels as the value, but any number can be substituted.

TRANSPARENT GIFS IN TABLES

One of the most important places to use transparent GIF files is within complex tables. For some reason, certain browsers won't accept an empty table cell and will automatically assign a value of 0 to the width and height of that cell. This is frustrating unless you use a transparent GIF file. Placing an element, even an invisible one, will prevent the browser from stepping in and overriding your height and width settings. Also, the images can be used to precisely position nested tables within their cells using the methods for vertical and horizontal white space explained before.

DESIGN CONCEPTS FOR TEXT

After you have laid out your page and are filling in the text, there are several issues you should consider, and these can often be handled with fairly simple extended HTML constructs. To produce a page that effectively conveys your message, carefully consider type treatments, the visual flow of body text, and effective use of colors and fonts.

USING TYPE STYLES

In its second version of Internet Explorer, Microsoft introduced the capability to specify typefaces in HTML. This was a watershed event in graphic design on the Web because it was the first of many extensions that empowered designers to better control the visual presentation of their content.

Developers have no way of knowing which fonts users will have installed, so they must specify a family of similar fonts in a particular order: if the first font is not available on the client machine, the browser will use the second or the third referenced font until it finds a match. Say, for instance, that you want to use Arial Bold for your headline, but you know that many Macintosh users will not have Arial installed. You would then specify that Helvetica be used as an alternative because it is substantially similar to Arial as a screen font and has been included with most operating systems for some years. You could include a font tag such as the following:

```
<FONT SIZE="5" FACE="ARIAL, HELVETICA" COLOR="000000">
<B> This is your headline </B>
</FONT>
```

The Arial/Helvetica set is a great standby when you need a reliable family of sans serif fonts.

Microsoft's Internet Explorer versions 2.X and above include support for type-face control in the <FONT> tag, as does Netscape 3.X and above. The lack of support in the 2.0 version of Netscape is problematic because many users had not yet upgraded at the time of this writing.

Microsoft also introduced a set of TrueType screen fonts called *WebFonts* that are designed for use in on-line content. This font pack is downloadable for free from Microsoft's home page (http://www.microsoft.com/truetype/). WebFonts are great to use because many Internet users have these fonts installed on their systems (Figure 1.5).

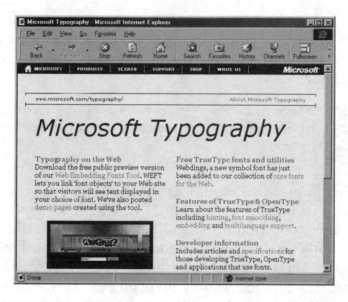

Figure 1.5 The Microsoft Typography site provides free fonts for Internet Users.

In addition to controlling the typeface displayed, the **<FONT>** tag allows control of the size, color, and other aspects of the text to which it is attached. This level of control allows designers to ignore the "procedural" tags such as **<H1>** and instead create their own text treatments for the varying levels within the informational hierarchy. We strongly suggest that you do this: the standard constructs for information description allowed by standard HTML are grossly inadequate and allow no control over how the browser will display the information. By creating standard text treatments for each level of heading and subsequent type styles, you can control the overall appearance of your document much more accurately than you can using HTML's standard "document description" metaphor.

The exception to the rule of ignoring the standard informational constructs is in CSS-heavy designs that map text styles to each tag. For more information, see Part II.

For example, you would use the `<FONT>` tag in this fashion to build a site in which you want to apply one type style to section titles, another style to subheads, and still another to body text. A good example of this kind of design is the Internet Nexus home page (Figure 1.6) at http://www.internet-nexus.com/main.asp. This site uses a specific font for section titles and the various levels of headers, varying type size and color according to a strict design concept. This is accomplished through conventional use of the `<FONT>` tag. A different font is used for body text, in this case, a standard Times New Roman, to contrast with the sans serif face used for the headings and titles. Take a look at this example and view the source code to get a good idea of how this was accomplished.

TEXTUAL DESIGN: THE FLOW OF INFORMATION

As you learned earlier, readers use the layout text to better understand the information presented and as an aid for more quickly and comfortably handling the flow of information. Concepts such as headers and subheads are part of this flow, but equally important is, once

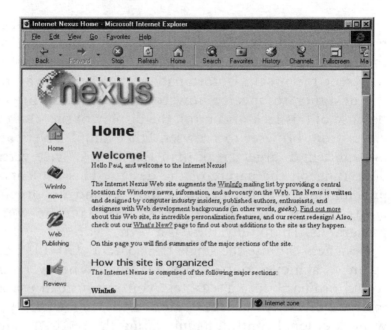

Figure 1.6 *The Internet Nexus home page uses explicit font declarations for a professional look.*

again, the use of white space. There exists a construct within the typesetting and desktop publishing industries called leading. *Leading* is the measurement of space from the baseline of one line to the baseline of the next line. This measurement, like the measurement of the text itself, is expressed in points and picas. Leading is an important aspect of the effective presentation of information. In HTML, however, no management of leading is provided so it cannot be approximated within body text. This is unfortunate but manageable because it is possible to specify leading between paragraphs and headings.

Traditional HTML handles leading between paragraphs with the ubiquitous <P> tag, which signifies the end of a paragraph and tells the browser how to represent the break. Unfortunately, there is no way for the designer to specify how to represent the break. Because of this lack of control, the display of the <P> tag varies from browser to browser. For example, Netscape may present a larger break than Explorer, or vice versa, depending on the nature of the design. This presents a problem in complex designs that depend on precise control over the amount of white space between paragraphs. Thankfully, there is a better way.

Designers can use the single transparent GIF file once again to achieve control over leading. Wherever you would ordinarily use a <P> tag, you can instead use an invisible GIF with a <BR> before and after where you want additional control, manipulating the HEIGHT value to control the amount of white space presented. For example, instead of

```
This is paragraph 1.
<P>
This is Paragraph 2.
```

You could use

```
This is paragraph 1.
<BR><IMG SRC="./images/pixel.gif" HEIGHT="12"
WIDTH="1"><BR>
This is paragraph 2.
```

This will allow you to tightly control leading. The level of control will be much less precise than that used in the desktop publishing industry and typesetting because there is no way to define font sizes. Without knowing the exact size of the characters presented, designers will not be able to specify an appropriate amount of leading. Still, this method provides more control than the conventional method.

COLORS AND FONTS

When the first desktop publishing applications arrived on the Macintosh, novice users often would take advantage of their newfound control over typefaces and styles by using several varying type treatments within the same page. This lead to some very gaudy designs. Remember that most effective designs use no more than two or three fonts. Now that the capability to control font size, style, and color has come to the Web, and the same thing is happening. Don't be a victim.

Instead, use this control to make your designs more effective. For the most part, this simply consists of specifying aesthetically pleasing type treatments for headers and subheads and using them consistently. Doing so will ensure that your designs are easy to read and interpret, and they will be visually appealing. Once you have embraced these ad hoc standards, it is time to take advantage of the rich text styles available in HTML.

Type styles, such as *italic*, **bold**, and <u>underlining</u> should be used sparingly and correctly. Bold type is used to make something **jump off the page**, to emphasize it. Italic type is also used for *emphasis*, but it has other, more specific uses. For example, book titles should be set in italic type, as should new terms that are being defined. Italic type was not available on traditional typewriters because a separate set of keys would have been required. Instead, underlining was used to present text that would be typeset in italics. Thus, underlining means italic, and hence should not be used. Underscoring this point is the fact that many browsers use underlining to represent links, so underlining unlinked text may confuse the reader. The answer is simple: don't use underlining.

 For more information about the correct use of type styles visit http://www.internet-nexus.com/web/design.asp. This page includes links, resources, books, and information that will help you to use type styles more effectively.

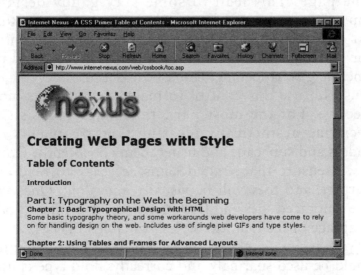

Figure 1.7 The Web design site at Internet Nexus includes more information about styles.

CONCLUSION

To sum up, Information design is an important part of creating a Web site. By intelligently laying out your pages and using white space and text effects correctly, your message gets across more effectively. Armed with the right tools and tricks, designers can create sites that adhere to information design theory without having to resort to using CSS technology, yielding sites that look acceptable in older browsers.

CHAPTER 2

Using Tables and Frames for Advanced Layouts

Tables and frames, both Netscape innovations, offer powerful workarounds to the limits of plain HTML by allowing the creation of complex layouts of both text and graphical elements. A few software companies have even leveraged some of these solutions to create software that allows WYSIWYG editing of Web documents with pixel-level accuracy of the layouts created. Although tables won't solve all your problems, they can be a powerful addition to a designer's toolbox, and understanding their use is imperative to advanced Web design.

HTML TABLES: THE DESIGNER'S GRID

When Netscape introduced the 1.1 version of its Navigator Web browser, it also added a powerful feature to Web publishing: HTML tables.

Tables are a simple construct for displaying tabular data or creating a complex layout for a Web page. Tables are easy to learn, and as you will soon find out, this feature was embraced by the Web development community as the foundation for layout on the Web. This book assumes knowledge of basic table creation. If you don't have any experience creating HTML tables, or want a refresher course, a tutorial is available in the Appendices of this book and on the Web at http://www.internet-nexus.com/web/cssbook/tables.asp.

 Although tables were initially a Netscape extension to HTML, they are now an accepted part of the language and widely supported. This de facto standard recently became the official word when the World Wide Web Consortium (W3C), the body that sets standards for HTML and the HTTP specification, made it part of the HTML 3.2 spec. (The 3.0 specification was never actually ratified. Officially, the Web went straight from 2.0 to 3.2.)

TABLES FOR COLUMN LAYOUT

When was the last time you read a magazine that had one column of text covering the whole width of the page? Graphic designers separate large bodies of text into narrow columns because it is easier to read large blocks of text when they contain 15 words per line or fewer. Longer lines make it more difficult for the reader to get back to the left margin and pick up the next line of text, often causing readers to lose their place and read the same line more than once. It is commonly accepted within the graphic design community that 9-13 words per line is best for optimum readability. This is a difficult standard to maintain on the Web where developers have little control over fonts and screen resolutions. Tables, however, can offer a limited workaround (see Figure 2.1).

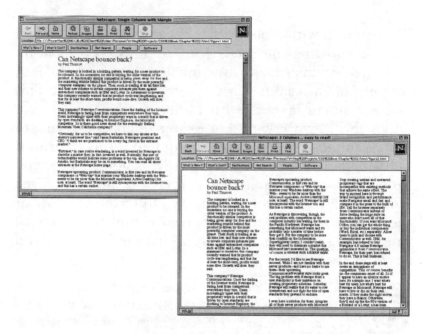

Figure 2.1 Tables offer limited column functionality.

The page shown in Figure 2.1 was created by building a simple table with one row and three columns. Notice the use of **CELLPADDING** to allow a 12-pixel "gutter" between the columns. Try some different width values and see what works in your design.

```
<TABLE CELLPADDING="12" BORDER="0">
    <TR><TD WIDTH="33%">
        Content for first column
    </TD><TD WIDTH="33%">
        Content for second column
```

```
   </TD><TD WIDTH="34%">
       Content for third column
   </TD></TR>
  </TABLE>
```

The problem with tables is that because you have no real way of knowing the user's font settings, you have no accurate way to estimate how much text to put into each column, often resulting in uneven column lengths. This makes column layouts with tables cumbersome if not impossible to work with. For example, imagine trying to put dynamic content into a layout like this. Without knowing how long each piece of text is going to be, you cannot construct a table that will lay out properly. Even worse, with no control over the width of the window or the exact size of the text displayed within the columns, these designs often look great in one browser and horrible in another.

 This lack of control has been the Achilles' heel of the Web design community since the first betas of Mosaic started showing up and is one of the primary focuses of the CSS specification. For more information on how CSS helps designers gain more control over point size and font display, see Part II: Web Design Matures: Welcome to Style Sheets.

FIXED-WIDTH TABLES FOR COMPATIBILITY

The solution to the problem of the varying widths of users' browser windows is to use fixed-width tables. By assigning an exact pixel width to each cell in a table, you gain more control over the final layout of the table, and in the end more control over the overall layout of the page. Large scale Web sites such as Excite, c|Net, and the Internet Nexus take advantage of fixed-width tables as a way to ensure consistent formatting across browser implementations.

Ordinarily, a table dynamically changes the width of each cell to accommodate the current width of the browser window. This causes problems when the layout demands a certain look and feel. By defining an exact width, the table will look the same no matter what width the user chooses to open the browser window, as shown in Figure 2.2.

```
<TABLE BORDER="0" WIDTH="600">
    <TR><TD WIDTH="150" ALIGN="CENTER">
    Navigational Buttons along the side of the screen
    </TD><TD WIDTH="450" ALIGN="LEFT">
    Here is the content for the page.
    </TD></TR>
</TABLE>
```

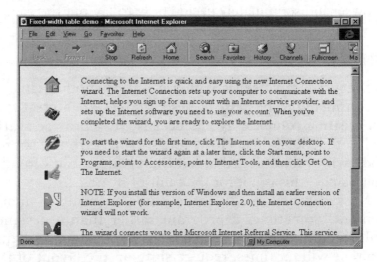

Figure 2.2 Fixed-width tables ensure that the page always looks the same.

One of the most important aspects of creating a fixed-width table design is deciding on an appropriate width for the primary table. First, consider the target audience. If your site is targeted at end users who are not technologically advanced, then a 600 pixel width is most often the answer because the "lowest common denominator" screen resolution on the Web is 640×480. When scroll bars and browser offsets are accounted for, just over 600 pixels of screen real estate is available to Web designers at this resolution. Also, 600-pixel tables print especially well from most browsers.

For sites targeted at advanced users, a 750-pixel table is often appropriate because more technical users tend to use screen resolutions of 800×600 or greater. Lower resolutions won't spoil the design with a fixed-width table; however, users will simply have to scroll to see the rest of the page. This is obviously preferable to having the browser indiscriminately decide how to lay out the page.

Using Nested Tables

Whenever a table exists within a cell of another table, it is considered to be *nested*. Nested tables are a great tool for creating complex layouts because they provide nearly unlimited flexibility. However, sorting through source code with tables nested several levels deep can often be confusing—this is not for the faint of heart.

Nested tables really shine when creating dynamic content. Sometimes a program rather than a designer will decide what content goes into a page, and this content will, at times, require shifts in the layout of the page. For example, let's say that you are retrieving content from a product database with two different types of content: basic products and featured products. The basic products might only contain a brief text description and some pricing information, whereas the featured products might go a step further by including a picture and a longer description. If you have written a program that dynamically creates HTML from the information in this product database, then it would be simplest to manage the layout of this content by using nested tables.

```
<TABLE BORDER="0" WIDTH="600">
   <TR><TD WIDTH="150" ALIGN="CENTER">
   <A HREF="/cgi-bin/navmap.map">
   <IMG SRC="./images/vert_navbar.gif" ISMAP></A>
   </TD><TD WIDTH="450" ALIGN="LEFT">
   <!- Insert records here ->
   </TD></TR>
</TABLE>
```

In this layout, the records are placed within a cell of this simple table. This works fine with a minor product:

```
<TABLE BORDER="0" WIDTH="600">
   <TR><TD WIDTH="150" ALIGN="CENTER">
   <A HREF="/cgi-bin/navmap.map">
   <IMG SRC="./images/vert_navbar.gif" ISMAP></A>
   </TD><TD WIDTH="450" ALIGN="LEFT">
   <H1> Basic Widget </H1>
   Basic Widgets are our simplest widget design. For
   widget shoppers on a tight budget this is the best
   solution!
   <H3> $19.95 </H3>
   </TD></TR>
</TABLE>
```

However, the standard products might require a more complex layout:

```
<TABLE BORDER="0" WIDTH="600">
   <TR><TD WIDTH="150" ALIGN="CENTER">
   <A HREF="/cgi-bin/navmap.map">
   <IMG SRC="./images/vert_navbar.gif" ISMAP></A>
   </TD><TD WIDTH="450" ALIGN="LEFT">
              <TABLE BORDER="0" WIDTH="425">
                    <TR>
                          <TD COLSPAN="3">
                          <H1>Super Widget</H1>
                          </TD>
                    </TR>
                    <TR>
                          <TD ROWSPAN="3">
                    <IMG SRC="./images/superwidget.jpg">
                    </TD>
                          <TD>Base Price:</TD>
                          <TD>$29.95</TD>
                    </TR>
                    <TR>

                          <TD>Batteries:</TD>
                          <TD>3.95</TD>
                    </TR>
                    <TR>

                          <TD> WidgetSafe&#153;
                          Warranty:</TD>
                          <TD>5.95</TD>
                    </TR>
              </TABLE>
   </TD></TR>
</TABLE>
```

As you can see, the table-within-a-table approach allows much more flexibility in the design without sacrificing simplicity.

Nested tables, although a powerful tool, can be dangerous in low memory situations. When working with complex nested table designs, make sure that your code is robust and that any designs with tables nested more than three levels deep are tested on a low-end machine with the minimum amount of memory allowed by the browser application. Complex nested tables can crash browsers that don't have adequate memory available.

CLOSE BUT NO CIGAR: WYSIWYG TOOLS

The advantage of *WYSIWYG*, or "What you see is what you get," tools is obvious: their graphical approach to design allows designers to concentrate more on the visual presentation and less on the creation of actual HTML code. On first inspection, it seems like these tools would be the answer to a designer's dreams, and in a sense they are. However, nearly all the WYSIWYG editors currently on the market miss the mark, often limiting the flexibility of the design and creating code that is cumbersome and hard to work with.

The Redwood, California-based company NetObjects created the first WYSIWYG editor that allowed pixel level control over the layout of elements within a page. This control is obtained through the creation of a complex grid of nested tables with precise height and width controlled by transparent images. This design flexibility comes with a price—paid in download time. HTML files created by NetObject's editor Fusion (Figure 2.3) can grow to 50–70 KB. This size is larger than all the combined graphic and text files on a well-designed site. Also, when using Fusion, designers are fairly well constrained to doing the things that the software lets them do easily. Although it allows a mechanism for the addition of elements not directly supported by the software, this mechanism is not very intuitive and suffers from spotty reliability. Even with these flaws, Fusion deserves a look as an example of what the next generation of Web tools will be like. With a rich set of site management tools and a simple approach to handling consistent navigational elements, Fusion is a great tool for beginning Web developers who want to get the job done quickly and easily but aren't all that concerned with the flexibility allowed by direct manipulation of code.

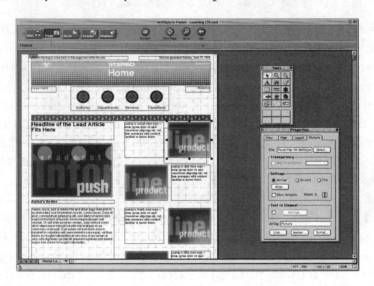

Figure 2.3 NetObjects Fusion provides pixel-perfect layout control, but sacrifices file size to accomplish this feat. Advanced site management tools make Fusion worth a look for beginning designers, though.

Advanced designers are probably breaking out their text editors, bloodied and beaten by the inadequacies of current graphical Web tools. But don't give up hope just yet, at least not if you are using a Macintosh. A company called GoLive has come out with a product called Cyberstudio that truly answers the collective prayers of Web developers everywhere. Unfortunately, this product is not available for Windows, and there are currently no plans to port Cyberstudio to the Windows platform. This is really too bad; Cyberstudio is a fabulous product.

What makes Cyberstudio such a good solution? It allows the unlimited flexibility of direct source code manipulation without sacrificing graphical layout capabilities. It allows pixel perfect layout control like Fusion but in controllable portions of the page so that designers can maintain some sanity in the file sizes of their HTML. Cyberstudio even has a visual tool for the creation of complex JavaScript coded—a first in a Web design program. Add to this rich feature set a powerful and attractive user interface, and you start to see why Cyberstudio is a clear winner. If you are a Mac-based designer who wants to create sites with ease, we strongly recommend that you check out Cyberstudio as shown in Figure 2.4.

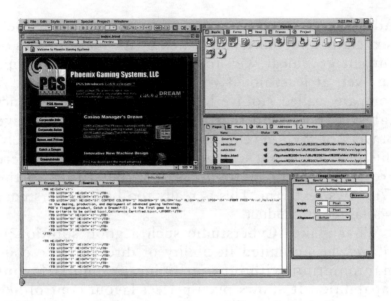

Figure 2.4 *GoLive's Cyberstudio provides a rich WYSIWYG environment for the creation and manipulation of Web pages without sacrificing the flexibility of hand coded HTML.*

FRAMED: SEPARATING CONTENT FROM NAVIGATION

Frames are similar in concept to tables, except that each cell is a separate scrollable "pane" that contains a unique URL. Frames can be targeted, allowing a link in one frame to affect another. This allows designers to create sites in which navigational elements are separated from the content—a boon to performance because these elements only need to be loaded and drawn once by the browser, as shown in Figure 2.5.

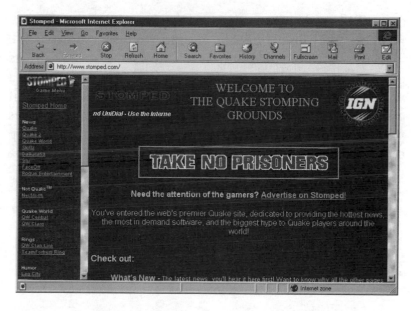

Figure 2.5 *Frames let Web designers separate navigational elements from the site contents*

The frames specification, which was submitted to the W3C for inclusion in future versions of the official HTML spec, was originally designed by Netscape Communications for inclusion in the 2.0 version of Navigator. Frames are fairly well supported; they are usable in Microsoft's Internet Explorer 2.X and newer and all subsequent versions of Netscape. Explorer includes a construct for *floating frames*, which are not constrained to the borders of the page, but this feature has not yet found widespread support.

The creation of a framed page starts with the creation of two or more *framesets*. These framesets each reference an HTML file that will be displayed in the frame. Frames, like tables, can be nested. In other words, the HTML file referenced within a frameset can contain its own framesets. (The specification is designed in such a way that loops created by a frameset referencing itself are automatically avoided.) Let's look at a simple frames page in which a navigational bar is available at the top of the page, as shown in Figure 2.6.

```
<HTML>
        <HEAD>
        <TITLE> Sample Frames Page </TITLE>
        </HEAD>
        <FRAMESET ROWS="80,*">
                <FRAME SRC="./nav.html" NAME="NAV">
                <FRAME SRC="./main.html" NAME="No Name">
        </FRAMESET>
</HTML>
```

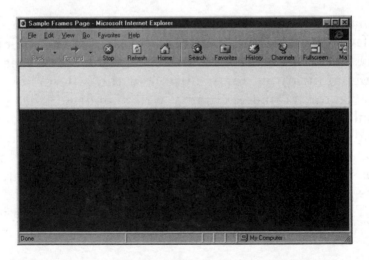

Figure 2.6 Frames are typically used to separate navigational elements from content.

Notice the size of the first frame is 80 pixels, whereas the size of the second frame is a wildcard character informing the browser to use the rest of the available window for display of this frame.

Framesets can be extended using a variety of extensions, including the capability to enable and disable scrolling in individual frames and a **NOFRAMES** tag enabling designers to create duplicate content for browsers that don't support frames.

 For more information on the frames specification, visit http:// www.internet-nexus.com/web/cssbook/frames.asp. This page includes a complete tutorial as well as links to various frames resources and examples on the Web.

Although frames provide a powerful tool to designers who want to create sites with a higher level of interactivity and application-style interfaces, they should be used sparingly. Frames often can confuse novice Web surfers who are confounded by the inability to bookmark framed pages effectively. (Creating a bookmark on a framed page will bookmark the frameset itself regardless of how far into the content the user has navigated.) Also, complex nested framesets can, much like tables, consume prodigious amounts of memory. Frames, however, are much more RAM hungry than their simpler cousins, so beware.

CONCLUSION

In summary, tables and frames are a worthwhile addition to any Web designer's bag of tricks. Once mastered, they can be combined to create advanced layouts and tightly controlled interactive experiences for your users.

CHAPTER 3

Microsoft HTML Layout Control

All this talk about tables and frames is well and good, but what if you want to create the following:

- Bleeding edge, multimedia Web pages
- Web pages overlapping objects
- Pages with control over the placement of elements on the canvas with precise, pixel-perfect positioning
- Graphical elements with advanced transparency effects and overlapping multiple background objects
- Truly interactive displays, with mouse-over effects and pop-up menus

One way to achieve these effects is to use Microsoft's HTML Layout Control, an ActiveX control that does all the above—and more. The problem with using the Layout Control is that it only works in Microsoft Internet Explorer 3.0 or newer, but with intranet sites where the IS department has some say over what browser users will have on their systems, or in dynamic sites where content appropriate to the user's browser is served, the Layout Control can be a compelling addition to a designer's toolbox, adding advanced layout and interactivity options to a previously static environment.

Microsoft has been collaborating closely with the World Wide Web Consortium, the body that helps define standards on the Web, to bring the power of the Layout Control to a wider audience. In fact, the W3C recently published a preliminary specification for incorporating similar layout functions to the HTML standard by incorporating some of these capabilities into the CSS specification. The HTML Layout Control is a preliminary implementation of this draft specification, so learning the control now will give you a taste of the future of CSS.

 For more information about future advancements in the CSS specification, check out Appendix C, The Future of CSS.

The Layout Control is an ActiveX run-time component that allows users to view Web pages that use these exciting new HTML extensions. In addition to enabling Web developers to take advantage of the new specification, the Layout Control supports fill WYSIWYG authoring of regions: the ActiveX Control Pad provides exact, coordinate control over object layout, layering, and transparency. Objects and elements can be placed within a region using strict height, width, and z-order attributes. The Layout Control then provides a preview implementation for using these regions within HTML documents viewed in ActiveX-enabled browsers.

The HTML Layout Control and the ActiveX Control Pad are both supplied for free from Microsoft and can be downloaded from http://www.internet-nexus.com/web/tools.asp.

LAYOUT CONTROL MAJOR FEATURES

Figure 3.1 shows a page designed with the HTML Layout Control.

Figure 3.1 *A Web page designed using HTML Layout Control.*

The major features of HTML Layout Control include:

- **Exact 2-D placement.** Controls can be placed exactly where the designer specifies within a 2-D region. Conventionally, the Web browser determines the placement of each element, but by using 2-D authoring and the HTML Layout Control, the designer gains new control, enabling consistency of the user interface and making it possible to build complex designs without resorting to bitmapped graphics that increase download time.
- **Overlapping regions.** The author can also specify the exact z-order of each control on the page. In the Figure 3.1, the box containing the "Breaking Grounds" text overlaps with part of the larger box containing the "Good Vibrations" image. Both of these regions are overlapped by the "Volcano Coffee" logo image.
- **Transparency.** The text label "Good Vibrations" is overlapping both the background and the large shaded box in the middle of the page. The text control that implements this label is transparent, so users can see through the text to objects underneath. Also, the cup (a Microsoft Windows metafile) is overlapped by the text label and is itself a transparent control overlapping both the background and large shaded box. Any ActiveX control that implements the ActiveX Control '96 specification for windowless controls can be transparent and used in this manner within the HTML Layout Control.
- **Scripting.** The HTML Layout Control also fully supports scripting, including both Visual Basic Scripting Edition (VBScript) and JavaScript. Thus,

any object contained in a 2-D region can script other objects in that region. In this example page, clicking the various label controls will cause the images within the region to change. Clicking other objects on the page causes navigation—switching the browser to a different page. In this example, the navigation is handled with VBScript.

DESIGNING 2-D-STYLE PAGES USING THE HTML LAYOUT CONTROL AND ACTIVEX CONTROL PAD

To assist in designing 2-D regions, Microsoft provides a free editing environment called the Microsoft ActiveX Control Pad. The ActiveX Control Pad is a WYSIWYG editing environment for embedding ActiveX controls in a 2-D region. Insertion of controls, including adjusting position, z-order, and properties of each control can be accomplished using a simple visual editor, similar in appearance to the form editor found in Microsoft Visual Basic. The ActiveX Control Pad supports automatic syntax generation of the tag used to embed objects in HTML pages. It also automatically generates CLSIDs that identify each object in the Registry, and property names and values for each object. A core collection of Microsoft ActiveX controls is provided with the ActiveX Control Pad, and other ActiveX-compliant controls can be added to the toolbox. Many of the supplied controls fully support the ActiveX Control '96 windowless control specification, providing authors with a rich palette of tools for creating next-generation Web pages.

The ActiveX Control Pad also includes a Script Wizard for VBScript and JavaScript, and an Object

Editor for placing ActiveX controls directly in the HTML stream without using a 2-D region. Refer to the Web site at http://www. internet-nexus.com/web/essays/ axcp.asp for more information on this tool. In addition, any text editor can be used to create pages using 2-D-style layout. Authors can simply follow the 2-D layout specification provided in this document. Finally, Microsoft also plans eventually to support WYSIWYG, 2-D-style HTML authoring in a variety of other authoring and development tools.

Together, the HTML Layout Control and the ActiveX Control Pad provide a set of tools for authors to build compelling Web pages. By itself, however, the HTML Layout Control presents a format for 2-D layout that other authoring tools can also support.

UNDERSTANDING THE HTML LAYOUT CONTROL

The HTML Layout Control (see Figure 3.2) represents a preview implementation of the draft W3C specification for 2-D-style layout in HTML. As a preview implementation, the HTML Layout Control specifies a separate file for objects placed in the 2-D region. This file is a simple text file that follows the preliminary W3C syntax. Objects inserted into the file are surrounded with the block tag, which is given a height and a width. The file is stored on the server and is read by the browser when the browser interprets the HTML Layout Control object in the HTML stream.

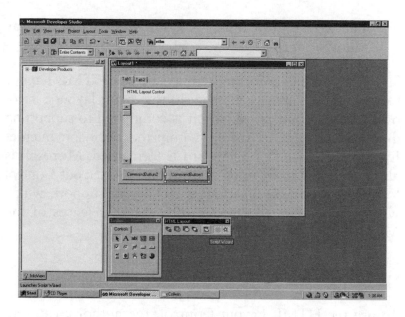

Figure 3.2 The HTML Layout Design view.

Supporting the 2-D-style layout format simply means following a few rules:

1. 2-D regions must be defined in a separate file. This file must be given an .ALX extension and is defined as part of the HTML Layout Control object tag within the HTML stream. (Note that after the W3C 2-D layout specification is finalized, Microsoft will support 2-D-style layout definitions directly within the HTML document rather than in a separate file.)
2. Objects defined within the 2-D region must be ActiveX-compliant objects.

3. The 2-D region must be enclosed within tags as follows: value WIDTH value"...

Supporting the 2-D format defined by the HTML Layout Control is a preliminary mechanism to provide layout control over ActiveX controls. Microsoft is committed to supporting the final specification natively within the Microsoft Internet Explorer after the W3C standard is formalized. Microsoft is also committed to ensuring that the HTML Layout Control format is compatible with future 2-D layout support, which will be incorporated directly into future releases of the Microsoft Internet Explorer.

USING THE HTML LAYOUT CONTROL

To use the HTML Layout Control, the author creates an HTML page and includes the HTML Layout Control in an **<OBJECT>** tag within the source code for the page. The author can optionally use the ActiveX Control Pad to more easily insert an HTML Layout Control (2-D region) within a new or existing HTML document.

This is a sample HTML file that includes an HTML Layout Control:

```
<OBJECT CLASSID="CLSID:812AE312-8B8E-11CF-93C8-
00AA00C08FDF
        ID="volcano"
        HEIGHT=444
        WIDTH=635
        STYLE="LEFT:0;TOP:0;WIDTH:640;HEIGHT:480">

<PARAM NAME="URL"
        VALUE="http://www.sample.com/sample.alx">
    </PARAM>
</OBJECT>
```

When instantiated, the HTML Layout Control defined by the tag will create a 2-D region within the HTML document. The 2-D layout file (.ALX file) used by this instantiation is referenced by the URL property with the VALUE "http://www.sample.com/sample.alx". This file contains the stored layout for the 2-D region designed by the author. The URL to this file is specified by the value of the URL property of the HTML Layout Control. This property is stored as a attribute on the tag of the Layout Control. The URL, tag, and attribute(s) are all automatically generated by the ActiveX Control Pad when inserting a 2-D region.

The size of the region will be the height and the width (in pixels) specified as STYLE layout-attributes on the tag, which is defined within the 2-D region (within the .ALX file). If height and width are also defined on the tag for the HTML Layout Control in the HTML stream, and the values for HEIGHT and WIDTH differ, the size of the layout will scale.

The tag is defined by the W3C as a block tag for division containment and is currently parsed by Microsoft Internet Explorer 3.0. The HTML Layout Control uses a single...block in the .ALX file to define a 2-D region.

The syntax for the tag conforms to the W3C standard, which is implemented by Microsoft Internet Explorer 3.0. See the W3C specification for the tag ("Inserting Objects," located at http://www.w3org/pub/WWW/TR/WD-object.html).

An HTML page can contain multiple HTML Layout Controls. Each 2-D region defined by a single instance of the HTML Layout Control behaves like other objects within an HTML page. 2-D regions can be placed in tables, aligned, centered, and so on. In this preliminary release, however, each instance of an HTML Layout Control is autonomous: No event or scripting within an HTML Layout Control can affect objects outside this region, and no event or scripting outside this region can affect the HTML Layout Control.

THE .ALX FILE

The .ALX file defines the fixed region and includes any scripts that would act on events and controls defined within this region. The region itself is defined with a tag. Script blocks can be defined before or after the tag within the .ALX file. This implementation does not allow script tags inside the tag to help ensure graceful forward compatibility with HTML standards and implementations.

The following outlines the attributes for the tag as used in this implementation. Although the .ALX file format does not support Cascading Style Sheets (CSS), the attributes specified on the tag are CSS style attributes that Microsoft anticipates, at the time of this writing, will be forward compatible with the future implementation of standard W3C HTML CSS. These CSS style attributes are specified with the **STYLE="LAYOUT:FIXED"** attribute.

The bare-boned structure of a .ALX file looks like this:

```
<DIV [ID=>name] STYLE = "layout-style-attributes"
   object-blocks
</DIV>
```

where direct attributes on the **<DIV>** tag are as follows:

AttributeDescription

ID	An optional ID attribute to identify the fixed region to scripting
STYLE	An inline style for tag (see STYLE attribute table below)

and attributes on the STYLE attribute are as follows:

STYLE AttributeDescription

LAYOUT	Must be defined as FIXED for a 2-D region
HEIGHT	Specifies the height of the layout region in pixels
WIDTH	Specifies the width of the layout region in pixels
BACKGROUND	Specifies the background color of the layout region in HEX digits

Any ActiveX control can be used within an .ALX file. This includes but is not limited to controls that implement the ActiveX Control '96 specification for windowless, transparent controls. A limitation of the HTML Layout Control is that no other type of **<OBJECT>** can be specified with the tag within an .ALX file. Tags defined outside the 2-D region are parsed by the browser, and in the case of Microsoft Internet Explorer 3.0, would conform to the defined within the W3C specification.

This is a sample .ALX file:

```
<SCRIPT>
sub MyButton_click
     Image1.zorder(0)
   end sub
   sub Image1_click
```

```
    window.location.href =
"http:\\www.mywebserver\gv.htm"
    end sub
</SCRIPT>

<!—Define A 2D Division—>
<DIV STYLE="LAYOUT:FIXED;WIDTH:635;HEIGHT:444;">
<!—Add Object blocks—>
    <OBJECT ID="MyButton"
STYLE="TOP:0;LEFT:0;WIDTH:808;HEIGHT:552;"
        CLASSID="CLSID:978C9E23-D4B0-11CE-BF2D-
00AA003F40D0">
                <PARAM NAME="BackColor" VALUE="794272">
        <PARAM NAME="Size" VALUE="21378;14605">
    </OBJECT>
    <OBJECT ID="Image1"
STYLE="TOP:144;LEFT:16;WIDTH:200;HEIGHT:192;"
        CLASSID="CLSID:D4A97620-8E8F-11CF-93CD-
00AA00C08FDF">
        <PARAM NAME="PicturePath" VALUE="
http\\www.mywebserver\drawncup.wmf">
        <PARAM NAME="BorderStyle" VALUE="0">
        <PARAM NAME="Size" VALUE="5292;5080">
        <PARAM NAME="VariousPropertyBits" VALUE="19">
    </OBJECT>
```

How Is the HTML Layout Control Distributed?

The HTML Layout Control is fully integrated into the final release of the Microsoft Internet Explorer 3.0 and 4.0 Web browser. Users can also download the HTML Layout Control separately from Microsoft, or automatically whenever they visit a page that uses the control. For users to view 2-D regions, they must have the HTML Layout Control installed on their computer, along with a browser that supports ActiveX controls, such as Microsoft Internet Explorer 3.0. The control can be freely redistributed by any customer or software vendor. Once installed, the HTML Layout Control does not need to be reinstalled as users navigate to subsequent pages that use 2-D layouts.

COMPATIBILITY AND FUTURE SUPPORT

As the W3C finalizes its specification for 2-D-style layout in HTML, Microsoft plans to incorporate support for 2-D layout directly into future versions of the Microsoft Internet Explorer, as well as a variety of authoring and development tools. After this support becomes native, the need for a separate .ALX file and HTML Layout Control will be eliminated. Their early preview implementation of 2-D layout for HTML follows the current W3C draft specification, and they expect to continue to work closely with the W3C as it moves forward with this specification. Microsoft plans to provide a conversion utility for the file format of the HTML Layout Control, if this is required by the final, adopted W3C specification for 2-D-style layout. This utility will convert Web pages created with the ActiveX Control Pad (or another editor) to be rendered in future browsers (such as Internet Explorer) that support 2-D layout with approved W3C standards. The utility will also integrate existing .ALX files directly into the HTML stream. This conversion utility will be free to the public.

CONCLUSION

The HTML Layout Control is a valuable tool for developing Web sites. Because it offers a peek into the future of the CSS specification, it is worth a look.

Now, armed with new knowledge of tables, frames, and the HTML Layout Control, you are ready to proceed into the world of CSS. You will start with a CSS primer, which introduces you to the basic concepts of the CSS specification. Then you move on into more targeted chapters about specific portions of the specification, including advanced selectors, font control, and white space control with CSS.

PART II:
WEB DESIGN MATURES:
WELCOME TO STYLE SHEETS

CHAPTER 4

A CSS Primer

As you may already know, HTML is a document description language rather than a page layout language. Why, then, does HTML have tags for bold, italic, and font selection if these things in no way affect the document's structure? An explanation is in order.

HTML *was* originally designed as a document description language, but when companies like Netscape started trying to distinguish their browser product from the pack, the path they chose was to extend HTML through the addition of tags that controlled layout rather than structure. As it happened, developers embraced the newfound control allowed by the new tags but not without a price. This price was paid in compatibility.

HTML, in its pure form, is inherently compatible. Not just in ways you currently think of compatible—HTML was designed from the beginning to be device independent. Instead of shooting for HTML to be available on either Mac or Windows computers, the original designers of HTML wanted it to be readable on any computerized device. These new extensions made HTML considerably less compatible because most of the new tags focused on presentation rather than document structure. CSS changes all this.

CSS allows designers to designate presentational information about the various structural elements within an HTML document. This works great, except for one minor detail: most HTML documents created by designers rather than computer scientists contain little information about the content's structure, instead focusing on how the browser is to *present* the content.

Because of this, the first step to learning Cascading Style Sheets is often to forget everything you know about HTML. Well, actually that's not entirely true—you do, however, need to forget everything you have learned about *designing* in HTML.

LEARNING DOCUMENT STRUCTURE

Before CSS, designers were forced to avoid the concepts of HTML document structure. Instead of using the conventional constructs for marking up content, designers were forced to use enhanced tags that only affected the presentation rather than the structure of the content. These are called *presentational* rather than *structural* tags.

The following is an example of a page designed using presentational tags:

```
<HTML>
    <HEAD>
        <TITLE>Joe's Home Page</TITLE>
    </HEAD>
```

```
<BODY>
    <FONT SIZE="4" FONT="ARIAL,HELVETICA">
    <B>Joe's Home Page</B>
    </FONT>
    <BR><BR>
    <FONT SIZE="3" FONT="Times New Roman">
    Welcome to my Home Page.
    </FONT>
</BODY>
</HTML>
```

Presentational tags allowed the designer to specify the typeface and size of the different sections, allowing much greater control over the presentation of the content than conventional HTML would allow. This same content in structural tags would look more like this:

```
<HTML>
    <HEAD>
        <TITLE>Joe's Home Page</TITLE>
    </HEAD>
    <BODY>
        <H1>Joe's Home Page</H1>
        <P>Welcome to my Home Page.</P>
    </BODY>
</HTML>
```

The code is much simpler and much more backward compatible with older browsers but doesn't allow for much control over design. It does, however, give much more information about the structure of the document.

The **<H1>** and **</H1>** elements tells us that the information contained within the tags is a level-one heading. The **<P>** and **</P>** tells us that the content is a body paragraph. This type of information is the structure on which designers can hang presentational information using CSS.

Let's take a look at that page, as it would be displayed in Netscape Communicator 4.01 for Windows NT (see Figure 4.1).

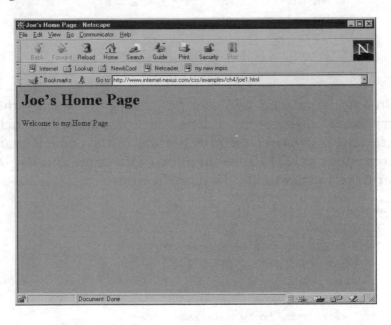

Figure 4.1 HTML Page displayed in Netscape Communicator 4.01 for Windows NT.

Now let's look at the same page displayed in Microsoft Internet Explorer 3.01 for Macintosh (see Figure 4.2). The first difference you notice is that Netscape renders the background in gray, whereas MSIE uses white. Second, you notice that the font weight and size are different, especially on the <H1> element. These differences occur because the browser is only provided with information about the structure of the information—the HTML contains no information about what the page should *look* like. What is needed is a way to create and apply a set of rules about how the different components of the document should be *presented*. This is where CSS comes in.

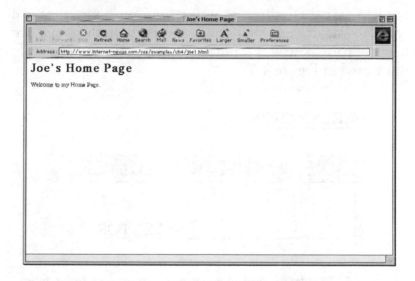

Figure 4.2 HTML Page displayed in Microsoft Internet Explorer 3.01 for Macintosh.

Different browsers often have different default background colors. For this reason, it is usually a good idea to specify the desired background color in your pages using either the <BODY BGCOLOR> attribute in HTML or the BODY {background: ...} element in CSS. Don't rely on "Netscape Gray" because "Mosaic Gray" is often a slightly different color.

In its simplest form, CSS is comprised of rules and style sheets. A style sheet is a collection of one or more rules that apply to an HTML document.

YOUR FIRST STYLE SHEET

CSS RULES!

In CSS, rules are simple *declarations* about how different types of content should be displayed. Each type of content is called through *selectors*. Let's say that we want to make sure that the body text of the page we used before is always black. We would use the rule illustrated in Figure 4.3.

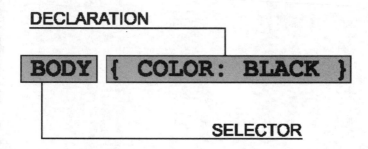

Figure 4.3 CSS rules are broken down into selectors and declarations.

The selector, in this case **BODY**, is an HTML tag that you want to take on the properties described in the declaration.

Declarations can be further broken down into *properties* and *values*, as shown in Figure 4.4. In this case, the property is COLOR, and the value is BLACK. Declarations are enclosed in {} brackets in much the same way that HTML tags are placed inside <> delimiters.

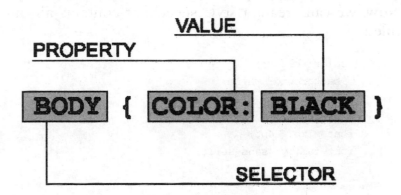

*Figure 4.4 CSS Declarations are broken down into
properties and values.*

Now that we have made sure that body text will be
black, let's make all the <H1> elements blue Sans Serif
font:

```
H1 { color: blue;
        font-size: 24pt;
        font-family: sans-serif;
    }
```

As you can see, we have mapped several declarations to
the H1 selector separated by semicolons. Let's do the same
to the BODY selector so that we can state the background
color:

```
BODY { color: black;
            background: white;
    }
```

Now, we can create a style sheet that contains all our rules:

```
BODY { color: black;
       background: white;
}
H1 { color: blue;
     font-size: 24pt;
     font-family: sans-serif;
   }
```

ATTACHING RULES TO HTML

Now that you have created these rules, it is time to attach them to the HTML. You can do this using the STYLE element. More information about attaching rules to a document is included in the next section.

```
<HTML>
   <HEAD>
      <TITLE>Joe's Home Page</TITLE>
      <STYLE>
           BODY    { color: black;
                     background: white; }

           H1      { color: blue;
                     font-size: 24pt;
                     font-family: sans-serif; }
      </STYLE>
   </HEAD>
   <BODY>
      <H1>Joe's Home Page</H1>
      <P>Welcome to my Home Page.</P>
   </BODY>
</HTML>
```

Now let's look at the same file in Netscape and Explorer (see Figure 4.5).

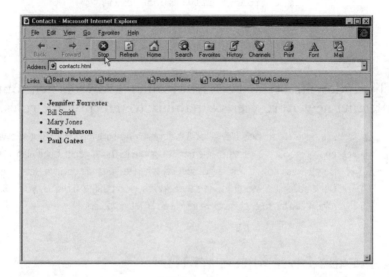

Figure 4.5 Style Sheets make display identical in both browsers.

As you can see, the rules within the STYLE–element were applied to the document, creating an almost identical display of the page in the two browsers. Congratulations! You have created your first style sheet design.

There is, however, one problem: browsers that don't understand style sheets will show, rather than interpret, the contents of the <STYLE> element. To avoid this, you can enclose the style sheet in an HTML comment.

```
<STYLE>
    <!--
        BODY    {
            color: black;
            background: white;
            }
```

```
H1       { color: blue;
         font-size: 24pt;
         font-family: sans-serif;
         }
   -->
</STYLE>
```

This hides the style sheet from older browsers without affecting newer browser's capability to interpret the rules.

 Although Netscape's Navigator 3.0 contains no support for CSS, it knows enough about the <STYLE> element to ignore it. This is good, but it also lulls developers into a false sense of security when testing their code in Netscape. Don't be fooled. Most browsers that don't support CSS will display your CSS rules if you fail to enclose them inside an HTML comment.

ATTACHING STYLE SHEETS TO HTML

In the preceding example, you created an HTML file and a style sheet and then linked them together using the <STYLE> element. There are several ways to accomplish this task, each suited for different situations:

- Embedding rules within the **<STYLE>** element
- Linking to a self contained style sheet file using the **<LINK>** element
- Importing style sheets using the **@IMPORT** notation
- Mapping rules on an element-by-element basis using the **STYLE**-attribute

THE STYLE ELEMENT

As you saw previously, the **<STYLE>** element allows developers a quick and easy method for including CSS rules directly within the HTML:

```
<HTML>
  <HEAD>
    <TITLE> The STYLE Element </TITLE>
    <STYLE>
       H1 {color: red }
    </STYLE>
  </HEAD>
```

In browsers that support the **<STYLE>** tag, the effect of the rules, rather than the rules themselves, are displayed on the page. However, a major philosophy in browser design is that a tag that is not understood is ignored. The problem is that some browsers, confused by the **STYLE** element, try to display the content of the style sheet. To avoid this, developers can place the style sheet within an HTML comment:

```
<HTML>
  <HEAD>
    <TITLE> The STYLE Element </TITLE>
    <STYLE>
       <!--
          H1 {color: red }
       -->
    </STYLE>
  </HEAD>
```

Although currently CSS is the only common style sheet language, the W3C has accommodated for the future development of new languages. The language used by the style sheet is then specified as an attribute of the STYLE element.

```
<STYLE TYPE="text/css">
```

It isn't necessary to include this information at this stage, but it doesn't hurt. Although it is logical to conclude that browsers will, for the foreseeable future, assume CSS if no other language is specified, one can never be sure what the future will hold.

THE LINK ELEMENT

Style sheets can also be saved as independent files, allowing them to be accessed from an unlimited number of HTML files through the **LINK** element. This method is especially good for large sites with many pages needing the same rules. All those pages could include a single line of code that would attach a site-wide standard style sheet to the page.

```
<LINK REL="STYLESHEET" HREF="/stylesheets/jrj.css">
```

The REL argument tells the browser that the file referenced is a style sheet, and **HREF** provides a path to the file to be used. The file referenced, in this case jrj.css is a simple text file including your CSS rules.

A great benefit of using this method is that the same HTML can be made to look dramatically different just by pointing to different style sheets. For instance, let's look at the same Joe's Home Page example using two different style sheets. The only change is the file name referenced within a LINK element.

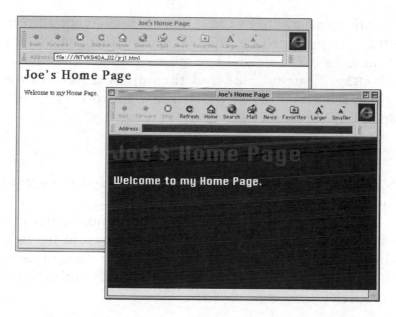

Figure 4.6 Using the LINK element to attach style sheets
provides flexibility.

THE IMPORT NOTATION

The Import notation is used when a designer wants to merge a style sheet with other style sheets for a more complete set of rules. This is discussed in more depth when cascading is explored in Chapter 7.

THE STYLE ATTRIBUTE

The **STYLE** attribute, not to be confused with the **STYLE** element, is used to apply a rule only once to a

specific element. For example, say that you want all your
<H1> elements to be blue except for one, which you
want to be red. You could create a style sheet that makes
all **<H1>** elements blue and then apply a declaration
within the actual tag in which you want to override the
document's style sheet:

```
<H1 STYLE="color: red"> This text will be red! </H1>
```

Notice that this is not a rule because the tag itself acts as
the selector.

This same effect can be accomplished more efficiently
using selector attributes, which are discussed in the next
chapter. Designers should, in general, steer clear of using
the STYLE attribute because it essentially defeats the
purpose of using style sheets.

INHERITANCE

Inheritance is the ability to inherit properties and
qualities from parental objects. This applies to people,
and as it happens, to CSS rules.

PARENT/CHILD RELATIONSHIPS

No, this section isn't about how to get along with your
kids, but rather the relationship of objects within a
hierarchy. When looking at an HTML document, a
hierarchy becomes apparent as shown in Figure 4.7.

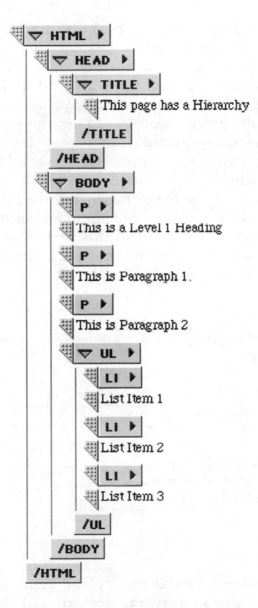

*Figure 4.7 An example of HTML hierarchy, as displayed in
GoLive Cyberstudio.*

As you can see, the **HEAD** and **BODY** elements are contained within the **HTML** element, and the various headings, paragraphs, and lists are contained within the **BODY** element. Stated in terms of parent/child relationships, **HEAD** and **BODY** are children of **HTML**, which is the parent. **BODY** becomes the parent when viewing elements farther down the hierarchy—the headings, paragraphs, and lists are children of the **BODY** element.

Even lower down the hierarchy are the list elements, which are children of the original **<UL>** element.

Developers often indicate this hierarchical system within their code by indenting items to represent their parent/child relationships:

```
<HTML>
    <HEAD>
        <TITLE> This page has a Hierarchy </TITLE>
    </HEAD>
    <BODY>
        <H1> This is a Level 1 Heading </H1>
        <P> This is Paragraph 1.
        <P> This is Paragraph 2.
        <UL>
            <LI> List Item 1
            <LI> List Item 2
            <LI> List Item 3
        </UL>
    </BODY>
</HTML>
```

Just as children inherit money and genes from their parents, elements inherit the properties of their parent elements. By that rationale, if you apply a rule using **BODY** as a selector, then it will be applied to all the children of the **BODY** element, including paragraphs, headings, and so on.

You override inheritance by applying rules down lower in the hierarchy. If you want all **BODY** elements to be black except for headings, you would create a set of rules such as the following:

```
BODY { color: black }
H1   { color: blue }
```

In this example, all elements of **BODY**, except for the blue H1 elements, will be black. This is because a more specific rule was applied to the **H1** elements, which overrides the more general rule applied to the parent.

USING INHERITANCE

A good example of where inheritance comes in handy is applying font styles to a document. In general, you want all your text to be the same color and font. There are exceptions of course—you may want your headings to be distinct from the rest of your text, and you may want to have **<BLOCKQUOTE>** elements take on a different style as well. Here is how you might create this effect:

```
BODY      { background: white;
            color: #02002B;
            font-family: Verdana, sans-serif;
            font-size: 12pt;
          }


H1        { color: #4D0002;
            font-family: Times, Serif;
            font-size: 36pt;
          }
```

```
BLOCKQUOTE { font-size: 14pt;
             font-style: italic;
           }
```

Notice that no font or font color was applied to the **BLOCKQUOTE** element; these declarations were inherited from **BODY**, the parent of **BLOCKQUOTE**. **H1**, however, has values that override the more general BODY element's rules. This illustrates the concept of inheritance perfectly: more specific rules always override more general rules.

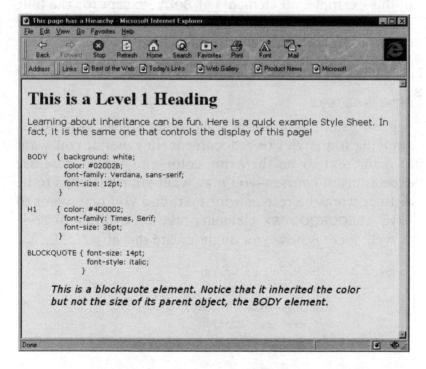

Figure 4.8 Inheritance in style sheets.

CSS GENETICS: WHICH PROPERTIES INHERIT?

Nearly all properties are inherited. However, some rules don't inherit because of practical reasons. The best example currently available is the **BACKGROUND** element because inheriting this property could be problematic for designers.

When you apply a background to the **BODY** element, for instance, you may expect that children of **BODY** would inherit the property, and it almost looks like they do. However, in reality, the child elements instead receive a "transparent" background, revealing their parent beneath. This allows for tiled images, which would otherwise not line up correctly. Figure 4.9 illustrates the problem by simulating the effect of an inherited background. (The background was manually assigned to the children of the **BODY** element in the second window.)

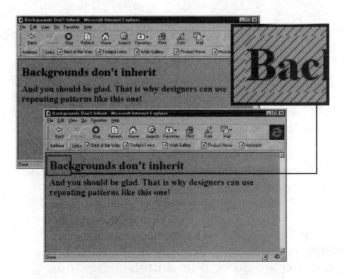

Figure 4.9 If the background property inherited, things wouldn't always line up correctly.

CASCADING

Now that you know a little about style sheets, you might wonder what the cascading part means. Style sheets are said to *cascade* because it is possible for a single HTML document to be controlled by a number of different style sheets.

There are several instances in which this may become an issue. For example, many CSS-capable browsers include a mechanism for users to create a default style sheet, allowing control over the display of pages that do not include rules of their own. In this case, the user's style sheet would be applied unless the displayed page explicitly sets rules to override the user's default settings. For example, say that the user has the following rule in her default settings:

```
BODY        { background: white;
              color: black;
              font-family: Verdana, sans-serif;
              font-size: 12pt; }
```

You have created a document with the following rule:

```
BODY        { background: gray;
              color: black;
              font-family: Times, serif;
            }
```

In this case, the **BODY** elements would take on the properties set by your rules: the background would be gray; the text would be blue and in Times font.

However, because you did not specify a font size, the user's default would be used. If you want, you can imagine that the browser creates a virtual style sheet from all rules. The browser merges the rules using a hierarchy of control with the user's default settings having the lowest priority, the linked or imported style sheets having a higher priority, and the local rules in the **STYLE** element having the highest priority.

Because the **STYLE** element has a higher priority than linked or imported style sheets, a designer could have a site-wide style sheet linked from all the pages in a site but still have the power to override the settings by using the **STYLE** element in certain instances.

Cascading is discussed in more detail in Chapter 7.

CONCLUSION

You now have a basic understanding of Cascading Style Sheets. You have learned about the basic principles of inheritance and cascading, and you know how to construct basic rules and attach them to HTML documents.

There is still much to learn. In the next chapter, we take a closer look at selectors.

CHAPTER 5

Complex Selectors

In Chapter 4, you learned that a CSS rule consists of a *selector* and a *declaration*. In the examples so far, the selectors have been references to simple HTML tags, but this isn't always the case.

The designers of the CSS spec understood that, to a designer, not all paragraphs are created equal—and as a result simply creating a single rule to govern the display of all paragraph elements like this:

```
P { font-family: 12pt Times, serif }
```

is sometimes inadequate. For this reason, they provided mechanisms through which designers can classify elements and specify rules throughout the classification. For special circumstances, even more specific overrides can be applied literally on an element-by-element basis.

These advanced selectors give designers more control and provide much of the power of CSS.

The four basic types of selectors are:

- *Type selectors* are the most basic—and most common—selectors. All the examples you have seen so far have used Type selectors.

    ```
    H1 { color: black }
    ```

- *Attribute selectors* allow designers to tack an additional attribute onto a tag and base rules on those attributes. Examples of these attributes are CLASS and ID, both of which are discussed in this chapter.

    ```
    .PRODUCTS { color: blue }
    ```

- *Contextual selectors* are sensitive to the context in which the rule is presented are sensitiveordered and unordered lists. Say that you wanted to display the first level of an unordered list in one style, but you want elements within that listythe children of the UL elementeto have a different style. You could assign a rule that only affects UL elements inside other UL elements.

    ```
    UL UL { color: red }
    ```

- *Pseudo selectors* are selectors that receive influence from outside factors. An example would be assigning colors to links and visited links. These selectors, referred to as *pseudo-elements*, will appear different based on whether the user has been to the site referenced.

    ```
    A:VISITED { color: blue }
    ```

TYPE SELECTORS

By far the simplest and most common selectors, Type selectors specifically call an HTML element. An example would be assigning a set of rules to **H1** elements: all **H1** elements would receive the properties described in the rule.

Type selectors can be grouped together in instances where several different types of elements need to be affected by the same rule. For instance, instead of creating redundant code like this:

```
P { color: black }
H1 { color: black }
UL { color: black }
```

You could instead create a rule with a list of multiple selectors like this:

```
P, H1, UL { color: black }
```

Both code blocks accomplish the same thing, but the second example is simpler, smaller, and, as a result, quicker to download.

ATTRIBUTE SELECTORS

Attribute selectors are used in rules that affect elements with the same attributes. Attributes are properties assigned within an HTML element. For example, *IMG* elements can have several attributes assigned to affect their display.

```
<IMG SRC="./file.gif"
    HEIGHT="25"
    WIDTH="25"
    ALT="Picture of my Dog"
    BORDER="0">
```

In the preceding example, the IMG element has five attributes assigned, each with a value. The **SRC** attribute is assigned a value that references a file, the **HEIGHT** attribute is assigned a numeric value, and so on. This same scheme of assigning attributes and values in HTML is used to create a more flexible selector mechanism for CSS through CSS-specific attributes.

THE CLASS ATTRIBUTE

In programming, it is often convenient to classify elements and make changes to all elements within a class. In fact, this logic gave birth to the concept of *object-oriented programming*. This same capability comes to CSS through the **CLASS** attribute.

The **CLASS** attribute allows you to classify elements, creating an easy way to modify groups of elements with a single rule. For example, suppose that you are creating a list of personal contacts.

```
<UL>
    <LI> Jennifer Forrester
    <LI> Bill Smith
    <LI> Mary Jones
    <LI> Julie Johnson
    <LI> Paul Gates
</UL>
```

Now suppose that you want to classify the contacts into personal and business associates and make the business associates appear in boldface print. You could do this manually by placing a **<STRONG>** or **<B>** tag in front of each business associate:

```
<UL>
    <LI><B> Jennifer Forrester </B>
    <LI> Bill Smith
    <LI> Mary Jones
    <LI><B> Julie Johnson </B>
    <LI><B> Paul Gates </B>
</UL>
```

This works, but CSS has a better way: create a **CLASS** for each type of contact and then apply the boldface type to that class (see Figure 5.1).

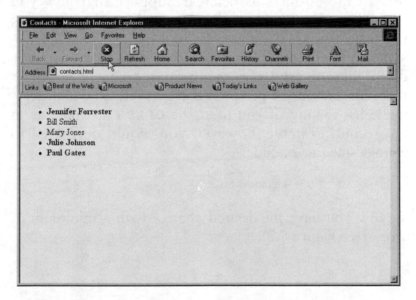

Figure 5.1 Business contacts are bold for emphasis.

```
<UL>
    <LI CLASS="BUSINESS"> Jennifer Forrester
    <LI CLASS="PERSONAL"> Bill Smith
    <LI CLASS="PERSONAL"> Mary Jones
    <LI CLASS="BUSINESS"> Julie Johnson
    <LI CLASS="BUSINESS"> Paul Gates
</UL>
```

This, along with the following CSS rules, would have the same effect:

```
.BUSINESS { font-weight: bold }
```

Notice the "." character before the **CLASS** name. It is the "flag" character that lets the browser know that you are referring to a **CLASS** attribute.

How is this better than manually assigning boldface text to the business associates? Suppose that now you want the personal contacts to appear in bold instead of the business associates. If you had manually included a **<B>** tag for each list item, you would need to manually delete the **<B>** tags from the business contacts and place them instead on the personal contacts—a tedious process if the list is long. If you used the **CLASS** attribute as in the second example, however, you would only need to change one line of code:

```
.PERSONAL { font-weight: bold }
```

Now you have the desired change with a minimum of work (see Figure 5.2).

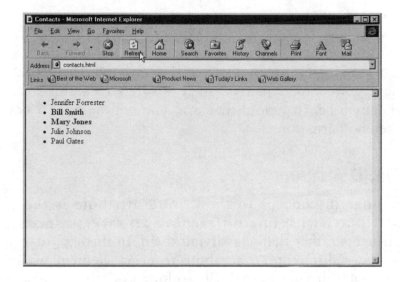

Figure 5.2 With one line of code changed, the emphasis is on personal contacts.

The names of **CLASS** elements must be one word, meaning that there can be no spaces. Underscores and hyphens are okay, but most special symbols are not allowed. In general, try to keep **CLASS** names short but descriptive. Some examples of good class names are as follows:

- NAMES
- people
- DiscontinuedProducts
- pub_files

The following names would not be allowed:

- NAMES! (contains special character)
- Discontinued Products (contains space)

The CSS1 Spec does not currently specify whether **CLASS** names are caps-sensitive, so it is safest to assume that they will be. (If indeed they are, you will be fine; if not, then no harm done.)

THE ID ATTRIBUTE

Similar in concept to the **CLASS** attribute is the ID attribute, with one difference: **ID** targets specific elements rather than classifying them. In theory, you can assign a different **ID** attribute to every element within the **BODY** of your HTML file so long as each **ID** value is distinct. This type of selector is valuable when you want to target a specific element in your HTML document:

```
<H1 ID="CompanyName"> Widgets, Inc. </H1>
```

Use of the ID attribute as a selector is similar to use of the **CLASS** attribute, except that the flag character is a "#" instead of a "." character:

```
#CompanyName { font-family: Impact, sans-serif }
```

In this example, Widgets, Inc. likes its company name to appear in its corporate font, Impact. You can easily accomplish this throughout your document:

```
<H1 ID="CompanyName"> Welcome to Widgets, Inc. </H1>
<H1>Quality</H1>
    Here at <EM ID="CompanyName">Widgets, Inc. </EM>
    we pride ourselves on quality. Our product line
    has always garnered critical acclaim, and commercial
```

```
success unmatched in the widget production industry.
This has always been a...
</P>
```

In the preceding example, the first **H1** element is the company's name, so it will appear in the specified font. The second **H1**, however, will be displayed in whatever font is assigned to **H1** elements. The **ID** attribute, being more specific, overrides the settings for **H1** elements.

The second instance of the **H1** attribute is when the company name is used within a body paragraph. Although Widgets, Inc. will again be displayed in the corporate font, the rest of the paragraph will be rendered in the default paragraph font.

THE STYLE ATTRIBUTE

The STYLE attribute is different from **CLASS** and **ID** in that it is used strictly as an HTML extension and is not accessed from a style sheet. Instead, it allows designers to apply CSS rules directly to an HTML element:

```
<H1 STYLE="color: blue; font-family: Times, serif">
Headline </H1>
```

As you can see, this allows the CSS declarations to be embedded directly in the HTML source. In a sense, this seems like you are creating rules without selectors, but in reality the element to which the **STYLE** attribute is applied becomes the selector.

In general, there are few instances where the **STYLE** attribute is useful. Because it flies in the face of one of CSS's most powerful features, the separation of presentation from content, it is counter-intuitive to designing CSS-enhanced sites.

CONTEXTUAL SELECTORS

Microsoft Windows 95 introduced a compelling feature to mainstream computer users: the concept of context-sensitive menus. This concept was not really new but had not yet seen widespread deployment in consumer-grade software. A *context-sensitive* menu appears differently depending on the element it is controlling. For example, right-clicking on a folder in Windows 95 produces the menu displayed in Figure 5.3, but right-clicking on an HTML file might produce the menu in Figure 5.4. The two menus are different because they only present options that are available relative to the object that is being controlled.

Figure 5.3 A context-sensitive menu from Windows 95.

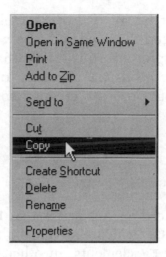

Figure 5.4 A *different context-sensitive menu from Windows 95.*

The concept of context sensitivity is important in CSS because of *contextual selectors*.

A contextual selector allows designers to create a rule that applies only in a given situationein the specified context. This is similar to an **IF** statement in many programming languages.

For example, say that you want all your text to be blue except for your **H1** elements and text that has been emphasized using the **<EM>** tag. You might create a style sheet like this:

```
BODY { color: blue }
H1, EM { color: red }
```

After applying this style sheet to a few of your HTML documents, you encounter a situation where some text inside an **H1** element is emphasized using **<EM>**:

```
<H1>NT 4.0 is a <EM>Powerful</EM> Operating System.</H1>
```

You realize that because both **H1** elements and **EM** elements have been declared red, the word *Powerful* is receiving no emphasis. You decide that you want **EM** elements *that are inside* **H1** elements to be blue so that they will stand out. You can create a contextual selector to do this job for you.

```
H1 { color: red }
EM { color: red }
H1 EM { color: blue }
```

Basically, the preceding rule states that **EM** elements that are children of **H1** elements should be blue rather than red like all other **EM** elements. In other words, make **EM** elements blue *within the context* of **H1** elements.

Notice that no separators are between the **H1** and the **EM**. Had there been a comma separating them, this would have simply assigned blue to **H1** and **EM** elements.

Another common use of contextual selectors is fine-tuning the display of list elements. Because lists are often nested, designers often want different looks for each level of the list. For example, this code will look like Figure 5.5 when displayed in Netscape Navigator 4.01 for Windows 95:

```
<H1> Contacts </H1>
<UL>
    <LI> Personal Contacts
    <UL>
        <LI> Bob Jones
        <LI> Cindy Smith
        <LI> Grace Allister
    </UL>
    <LI> Business Contacts
```

```
<UL>
    <LI> Widgets, Inc.
    <UL>
        <LI> Jim Johnson
        <LI> Joe Ray
    </UL>
    <LI> Acme, Inc.
    <UL>
        <LI> Bill Jenkins
        <LI> Amy Brown
        <LI> Jana Wesley
    </UL>
    </UL>
</UL>
```

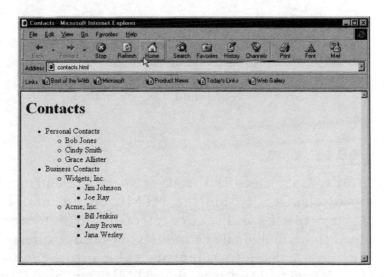

Figure 5.5 A nested list.

Through the use of contextual selectors, you could assign a different set of display properties to nested list elements:

```
UL UL { font-weight: bold }
```

This would make all nested list elements bold. The rule, however, would not affect the first level of the list, as shown in Figure 5.6.

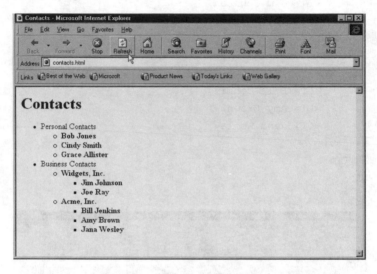

Figure 5.6 Only nested list items are affected.

PSEUDO SELECTORS

Generally, CSS selectors specify a specific element or group of elements within the HTML document. The exception to this is Pseudo selectors, which were designed to accommodate certain layout needs expressed by designers. Pseudo selectors take into account information not included in the HTML source code in applying CSS rules.

There are two major examples of pseudo elements: *pseudo elements* and the **ANCHOR** *pseudo-class*.

PSEUDO ELEMENTS

Two examples of pseudo elements are the first-line and first-letter elements. Neither of these elements exists in the document's structure or code. Rather, they are concentrated on the presentation of textual content.

 The current specification for CSS does not require support of pseudo elements for full compliance, so there is no way of knowing what kind of support these features will see. Indeed, neither Netscape nor Microsoft's 4.0 browsers provide support for pseudo elements.

Both these elements exist to service designer's needs to duplicate the rich layout control they are used to in conventional print-based publishing. Magazines, books, and other printed materials often take advantage of a typographical effect called drop caps—when the first letter of a section of text is made larger than the rest of the text and set into the text block, as shown in Figure 5.7.

Drop caps are attractive and are common in printed documents. Before CSS, Web designers would create the drop cap as an image file and use the **ALIGN="LEFT"** attribute to create the "dropped" effect. This technique was visually convincing, but it was not without drawbacks. For instance, images take longer to download than text, and users often surf with image downloading turned off or use browsers that don't support inline images.

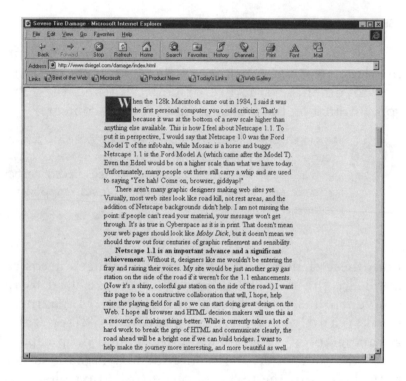

Figure 5.7 A drop cap effect is an effective design trick.

A better approach was needed and is supplied by CSS through the first-letter pseudo element.

Suppose that you want to achieve the same effect that exists in Figure 5.7 without the image. The first step is to enlarge the size of the first letter of the paragraph using the first-letter element. Notice the colon character is used as the flag for pseudo elements:

```
P:FIRST-LETTER { font-size: 400% }
```

Upon further reflection, you decide you don't want drop caps on every paragraph. You decide to create a class of

paragraphs that will receive the drop cap effect. The code
changes to the following:

```
P.DROPCAP:FIRST-LETTER { font-size: 400% }
```

Now you need to make the enlarged letter drop into the
body of text, or "float" the same way that the image did
when you assigned **ALIGN="LEFT"** to it. You will use
the CSS float property, discussed in detail in Chapter 7.

```
P.DROPCAP:FIRST-LETTER { font-size: 400%; float: left }
```

Now you have a perfect drop cap (see Figure 5.8), and
the effect is nearly identical to the image-based effect
shown in Figure 5.7!

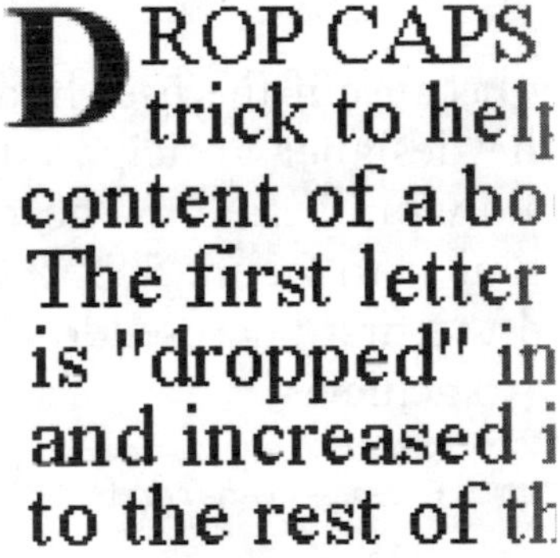

DROP CAPS
trick to help
content of a bo
The first letter
is "dropped" in
and increased i
to the rest of th

Figure 5.8 CSS *allows drop caps without images.*

A common effect in old books was to combine drop caps
with all uppercase letters on the first line.

There is really not an easy way to do this in HTML because designers have no reliable way of knowing what point size the text on user's browsers will be and to what size their browser window will be opened. Because text auto-wraps when the window is resized, this presents a dilemma to designers who want to achieve this effect.

The only way to create a design where the first line of text was in all uppercase letters was to place hard breaks in the code so that you could control the layout of the text:

```
<IMG SRC="./dropped_C.gif" ALIGN="LEFT" ALT="C">
ASCADING STYLE SHEETS ARE A NEW DEVELOPMENT IN THE<BR>
web design industry- allowing greater control then<BR>
previously available to HTML hackers across the net,<BR>
CSS is being heralded as the most important
evolution<BR>
to web design since HTML tables were introduced by<BR>
Netscape Communications.<BR CLEAR>
```

This was clumsy because if the user had a larger default font size than the designer anticipated, or a narrower screen, lines would wrap before the hard breaks, and the effect would be similar to Figure 5.9.

Using CSS and the first-line pseudo-element, however, this effect is easy to achieve:

```
P.DROCAP:FIRST-LINE { text-transform: uppercase }
```

No hard breaks are needed because the browser will interpret and display the first line transform based on the current view. If the user resizes the window, the text will wrap, but the effect will not be lost. The effects of this code are seen in Figure 5.8.

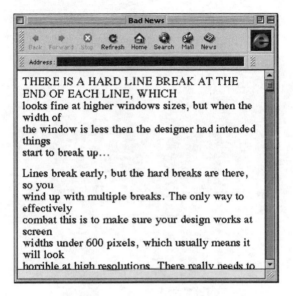

Figure 5.9 Attempts to hard-code breaks into HTML were often disastrous.

CHAPTER 6

Fonts in CSS

Most of the CSS specification is dedicated to controlling the display of text. This is good because Web sites themselves mostly contain text.

The effective control of typefaces and fonts entered the world of mainstream computing with the introduction of the Apple Macintosh in 1984. Prior to the Mac, computer systems ranging from Gary Kildall's CP/M to Tim Patterson's Q-DOS (and subsequently, MS-DOS) used a single monospaced font, often with only one available case.

When the designers made a commitment to extending type control on the Mac, they looked to the publishing industry for convention, and in doing so, inadvertently empowered the creation of an entire industry: desktop publishing, or DTP.

CSS ROOTS IN DESKTOP PUBLISHING

The typographical conventions used by CSS are mostly based on existing desktop publishing conventions. Why is this an issue if DTP is based on conventional publishing? Because DTP is a *subset* of conventional publishing. Although the two are similar, DTP contains only a small part of conventional publishing terminology and techniques. After all, publishing has evolved over the hundreds of years that have passed since the introduction of the printing press, but DTP has had less than 15 years to reach its current level of maturity.

Because of CSS's roots in desktop publishing, it is approachable to developers familiar with DTP terminology. Even those without any substantial DTP experience will be able to quickly grasp the fundamental typographical properties used by the CSS specification. Those with backgrounds in traditional publishing, however, will need to understand some basic differences between their world and the digital space in which CSS is developing.

FONTS VS. TYPEFACES

In traditional publishing, a *typeface* is a particular *style* of type. For instance, Times New Roman is a typeface, as is Helvetica. Typefaces, often called *faces* for short, can include different versions of each character, to represent bold or italicized type, for instance. *Fonts*, however, are one specific size and variation of a typeface. Times New Roman Bold 12 pt., by that rationale, is a font, and Times New Roman Bold 14 point is a separate font altogether. This is because in traditional typesetting each size and variation of a typeface must be individually manufactured and stored separate from other fonts so that they wouldn't get mixed up. In DTP, however, PostScript and TrueType fonts are stored on a computer, can be easily scaled to any size, and variations can be created by the computer by using simple algorithms. In desktop publishing, the terms font and typeface are often used interchangeably; the same is true in CSS.

 Even the Mac didn't always have truly scalable fonts. In the beginning, fonts were stored as bitmaps for each size and style. Now, with TrueType and PostScript font technologies, this is no longer necessary. Although bitmap fonts are still in use, they are rare and aesthetically inferior to the newer technologies.

MEASURING TYPE

Type is generally measured in *points*, abbreviated as "pt." (as in 14-pt.). Points come from traditional publishing, but in DTP the definition of point is much more narrow. Although there are three different point sizes in publishing, DTP almost always uses a single size, which is 1/72 of an inch. Because DTP evolved first on the Mac and the Macintosh Operating System had defined a standard of 72 pixels per inch, this size point was convenient: a 12-pt. font was also a 12-pixel font.

 The resolution of Windows displays is assumed to be between 96 and 100 dpi, so type will often appear to be slightly different sizes between platforms.

FONT SIZES

To measure type, you first must define the parts of a letter. For example, look at the letters shown in Figure 6.1. When you were first learning to write, you probably formed your first letters on special paper that had a set of lines to guide you towards consistent letter sizes. Usually consisting of three lines, these guides represented the *ascender*, *x-height*, and *baseline* of your letters. The only missing element was the *descender*.

Figure 6.1 The parts of letters.

The ascender is the highest part of any letter. Most uppercase letters span from the ascender to the baseline, which is the imaginary line on which the type sits. Lowercase letters often drop below the baseline, creating a descender, or the lowest part that a letter can extend below the baseline. The main body of lowercase letters extends to the x-height, whereas some letters will have parts that reach up to the ascender. Type is measured from the top of the ascenders to the bottom of the descenders, so 12-pt. text is 12 points from the top of an uppercase *T* to the lowest point on a lowercase *g*.

The visual perception of a font's size can be dramatically changed based on the distances between each imaginary line. The paragraphs shown in Figure 6.2 are both rendered in 14-point text, but the one on the left appears to be larger. This is because the letters have large x-heights and comparatively small ascenders and descenders. Both are the same point size, though, because the measurement from ascender to descender is the same. This visual discrepancy between different fonts should be considered in your designs. The *leading*, (pronounced "ledd-ing") or vertical spacing, will feel much tighter in fonts that have large x-heights, so you may want to use extra leading in your designs.

 For more information on controlling leading check out Chapter 11.

OTHER MEASUREMENTS

You can also use character width to measure type. In proportionally spaced fonts, each character uses a different amount of horizontal space. For example, an *i* is usually narrower than an *m*. To measure the width of type, CSS has two methods, both based on the vertical type size: the em unit and the ex unit.

The Em Unit

In CSS the em unit (or simply "em")is the same as the point size. One em unit in 12-pt. text, then, is 12 points. In DTP and traditional publishing, the em unit can have various meanings: sometimes, it refers to the width of a lowercase *m* in a particular font for example. In CSS, however, an *em* is always equal to the point size of the text. The advantage of the em unit's availability becomes more obvious in practice. Say that you want to indent each paragraph one em unit. In regular HTML, you might do something like this:

```
<FONT SIZE="3">
<IMG SRC="pixel.gif"
```

```
WIDTH="12"
HEIGHT="1">
Here is the beginning of the paragraph...
```

The font size of 3 usually refers to 12-point text, which is generally close to 1 pixel per point. That is a carefully qualified sentence that basically means "it might kinda maybe sorta work."

If the user has a font size other than 12 points set as the default size or is running a screen resolution that makes his display more or less than 72dpi, you have a problem. The indentation will not correspond to the actual text size.

However, if you create an indentation of one em unit in CSS, it will scale with the point size of the text. An em unit in a block of 12-point text will always be 12 points; a 24-point em unit will always be 24 points.

The Ex Unit

The *ex unit* in CSS is equal to the x-height of the font. Although you can explicitly set the size of an em unit (by specifying the point size of the font), you cannot control the ex unit's size because the x-height differs between fonts. Generally, the ex unit is less useful than the em unit.

CLASSIFYING TYPE

CSS typefaces are classified into five categories:

- Sans serif
- Serif
- Monospaced
- Cursive
- Fantasy

Almost all typefaces fit into one of these categories.

Just What Is a "Serif"?

A *serif* is the decorative cross stroke contained in some typefaces. Typefaces are classified based on whether they contain serifs. A font with serifs is called a *serif font*, whereas a font with no serifs is called a *sans serif font*. An example of a serif font can be seen in Figure 6.2.

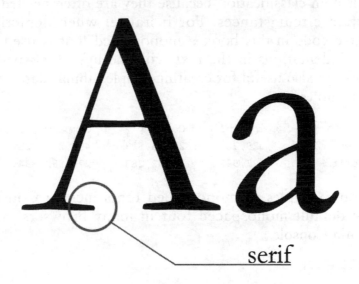

serif

Figure 6.2 A serif font.

Times New Roman is a serif font, which is the default typeface used in most browsers. Examples of sans serif fonts include Helvetica and Arial, which are popular fonts distributed with most operating systems.

Proportional vs. Monospaced

The first personal computers used *monospaced* fonts, or typefaces in which every character occupies the same width. Typewriters typically use monospaced fonts. In publishing, however, typefaces were designed for maximum readability, so each letter is designed to take up only as much space as it needs. This type of font is said to be *proportionally spaced*. In a proportionally spaced font, an *I* is much narrower than an *M*.

Both monospaced and proportionally spaced fonts can be either serif of sans serif, but monospaced fonts receive their own classification because they are often needed in certain circumstances. For instance, when depicting source code in this book a monospaced font is used so that indentations in the text will line up. Monospaced fonts are also useful for creating simple tabular data, like basic tables.

```
           Company 1     Company 2     Company 3
Sales      1,029,923     2,293,823     433,285,923
Profits      523,992     1,002,283     223,932,834
```

Good examples of monospaced fonts include Courier (the default monospaced font in many browsers) and Lucida Console.

Cursive Type

Cursive refers to typefaces designed to resemble handwritten text. Cursive letter shapes are often more rounded and decorative than serif or sans serif fonts, and as a result are usually more difficult to read. For this reason, cursive text is seldom used for large blocks of body text, instead being reserved for headlines and display purposes. Good examples of cursive fonts include Brush Script, Vivaldi, and Comic Sans.

Fantasy

Fantasy fonts are designed specifically for display purposes and are often far too unusual for use in body text. Much more decorative than cursive fonts, fantasy typefaces are often irregularly shaped and extremely difficult to read in large quantities. Some fantasy typefaces don't even include a full alphabet or complement of special characters. Poplar, for instance, which is used heavily on the Hip Mama site (http://www.hipmama.com) doesn't include apostrophes or commas, but it is an interesting font useful for headlines and graphical elements. Hip Mama is shown in Figure 6.3

Figure 6.3 *The Hip Mama web site uses a fantasy font, Poplar, for its logo.*

Examples of fantasy typefaces include Impact, Engraver (or its cousin Copperplate), and Revue.

WHY CLASSIFY FONTS?

CSS typeface classification gives designers a tool for describing how to choose an appropriate font substitution should the specified font not be available to the user's browser. For example, if the designer specifies New York as the typeface, but the New York font isn't installed on the user's system, the browser will choose a substantially similar serif font, usually Times New Roman.

The default fonts that two browsers use for each classification often leave users scratching their heads. Just so that you know what to expect, here is a table of each browser's default typeface for each generic font family:

FONT FAMILY	Netscape Navigator/ Communicator 4.X (Windows)	Netscape Navigator/ Communicator 4.X (MacOS)	Microsoft Internet Explorer 4 (Windows)	Microsoft Internet Explorer 3 (Windows)	Microsoft Internet Explorer 4 (MacOS)
Serif	Times New Roman	Times	Times New Roman	Times New Roman	Times
Sans serif	Arial	Times	Arial	Arial	Times
Cursive	Arial	Times	Comic Sans MS	Comic Sans MS	Times
Fantasy	Arial	Times	Ransom	Ransom	Times
Monospace	Courier New	Times	Courier New	Courier New	Monaco

Why do the browsers use such inane default settings? We'll probably never know. However, being aware of the defaults allows you to plan accordingly and make sure that things will look okay in all browsers. All these browsers allow the user to change the defaults, but few users take advantage of this feature.

TYPE STYLES

Type styles, such as bold and italics, are allowed in HTML, but developers taking advantage of CSS have much more control over these attributes. Whereas in HTML you can specify that a certain passage of text be displayed in boldface, in CSS you can declare the exact weight that the text should be displayed as a number between 100 and 900:

```
H1 { font-weight: 700 }
```

Of course, you can also use less specific declarations:

```
H1 { font-weight: bold }
```

 Controlling font weight is discussed in more detail in the next section.

CONTROLLING FONTS WITH CSS DECLARATIONS

This section contains the meat of the CSS specification: the available properties and values associated with the control of type. You may want to use it as a reference later when creating your style sheets. Each font and text property will be presented with all available values and a couple of examples to illustrate its use. Additionally, any notes about the use of a property, such as properties that are not inherited, are discussed.

FONT-FAMILY

Any font can be used as an initial value, but you should generally use common fonts that are likely to be installed on a user's system. A good place to start is with the fonts installed by default with the Windows operating system, or with Microsoft's WebFonts, a set of freely downloadable TrueType fonts available from the Microsoft Typography Web site at http://www.microsoft.com/type/. Much like the **FONT FACE** attribute in HTML, you can specify a list of possible fonts in order, separated by commas.

```
H1 { font-family:Arial, Helvetica }
```

For font names that have special characters, names can be enclosed in quotation marks to ensure that no confusion is created by the characters.

```
H1 { font-family: "Old-Town" }
```

Additionally, a generic *font family*, or font classification can be specified. The five possible values are serif, sans serif, monospaced, cursive, and fantasy. This is placed after all specific fonts and is used as a last resort if none of the specific fonts can be found.

```
H1 { font-family: Arial, Helvetica, sans-serif }
```

 Generic families cannot be enclosed in quotation marks. This is so that the browser doesn't assume that you want a font called Fantasy instead of the generic fantasy classification of fonts.

FONT-STYLE

The *font-style property* allows control over the style of the font. The available values for the font-style property are normal, italic, and oblique. Notice that "bold" is conspicuously absent as an available font style because CSS provides a different mechanism for the control of font weight, which is the next property discussed.

```
EM { font-style: italic }
```

Normal text is the default value of font-style, which is to say that if no font style is specified, normal is used.

Oblique is a slanted version of the normal font, usually slanted to the right. Italic type is similar but not necessarily the same thing. Italic type is often designed separately from the normal text, especially in serif fonts. Figure 6.4 illustrates the difference between Oblique and Italic type.

Italic

Oblique

Figure 6.4 Italic type is often different from Oblique text.

FONT-WEIGHT

The *font-weight property* controls the weight of the font. The value of the font-weight property can be expressed as a descriptive term or a numerical value.

Available values are lighter, normal, bold, and bolder, with the default value being "normal."

Available numeric values are 100, 200, 300, 400, 500, 600, 700, 800, and 900. Because values in between are not valid, some developers question why a three-digit number is used rather than a single digit. Only the developers of the specification know for sure.

 At least thatís the way it is *supposed* to work. In reality, Explorer 3.0 doesnít support numeric values, and Navigator 4 for MacOS doesnít support keywords such as *bold* and *lighter*. Sometimes you just canít win.

With the numeric values, the smaller the number the lighter the text. Normal text is 400, 700 is the equivalent of bold text. Not all fonts provide variants for other numbers, but some, including multiple master fonts, include versions for all nine values (Figure 6.5). If no variant is available for the specified value, CSS substitutes the closest available variant. For example, if you specify a value of 800 for a font that doesn't include variants for that value, the browser substitutes a value of 700, or regular bold text.

font-weight 100
font-weight 200
font-weight 300
font-weight 400
font-weight 500
font-weight 600
font-weight 700
font-weight 800
font-weight 900

Figure 6.5 The font-weight property's nine numeric values.

FONT-VARIANT

The *font-variant property* is used to specify display of text in "small-caps." The only two values available are small caps and normal, with normal being the default. It is safe to assume that future versions of the CSS will provide additional properties to the font-variant property; otherwise, the designers of CSS would probably just used small caps as a value for the font-style property.

```
H1 { font-variant: small-caps }
```

Small-caps are used frequently in graphic design and are a very effective design tool. In small caps, lowercase letters are represented by smaller versions of the uppercase letters. Some fonts, such as Copperplate, only offer a small-caps version, whereas others don't provide a small-caps version. When no small-caps version is provided, CSS simply scales down the uppercase letters, creating an effective substitute for true small-caps. (The difference really isn't noticeable at most screen resolutions, but can be spotted quickly by an experienced designer when outputted to a high-quality printer.) The effect of small caps is illustrated in Figure 6.6.

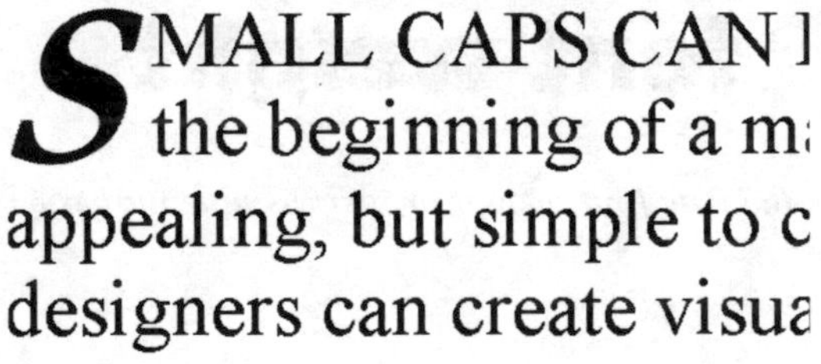

*S*MALL CAPS CAN]
the beginning of a m:
appealing, but simple to c
designers can create visua

Figure 6.6 Small caps are an effective design technique.

Before CSS, the only way to create small-caps was to type all the content in uppercase letters and increase the size of caps with the FONT SIZE attribute:

```
<FONT SIZE="6">S</FONT><FONT SIZE="4">MALL <FONT
SIZE="6">
C</FONT><FONT SIZE="4">APS USED TO BE A MAJOR PAIN
```

This approach had several problems. First, it created incredibly cumbersome source code. Even worse, the only way to change the case of text in many text editors is to re-key it, a major problem with large bodies of text.

You now can change case easily in CSS using the text-transform property, discussed later in this section.

FONT-SIZE

The *font-size property* is pretty self explanatory. It controls the font size. However, the methods for specifying sizes in this property are widely varied.

The values in the font-size property can be expressed as absolute, relative, or percentage. Alternatively, size can be specified as a "length."

Absolute Sizes

Absolute sizes reference a table of sizes kept within the browser. The values available are xx-small, x-small, small, medium, large, x-large, and xx-large. Obviously, each is a step up in size. The CSS specification states that each step can create an increase in size no greater than a factor of 1.5. However, so long as this maximum is taken into account, the actual difference between each step is left to the browser. This allows users to set a preference for a base font size. Visually impaired users can specify an unusually large base font size, and fonts scaled using absolute sizes will be scaled in relation to that base size.

```
H1 { font-size: x-large }
```

Relative Sizes

Relative sizes, like absolute sizes, allow the declaration of size to be a keyword. However, in relative sizes, the value is in relation to the parent object rather than the table of sizes in the browser. Available relative values are "larger" and "smaller"

For example, let's say that you have specified that all body text should be displayed using the absolute value of "small," but you want **BLOCKQUOTE** elements to be displayed in smaller text. You could use a rule like

```
BLOCKQUOTE { font-size: smaller }
```

to accomplish this. The key factor here is that the values are in relation to the values of the parent object, or to the inherited value. If you later changed your style sheet to say that all body text would be displayed as large text rather than small text, the relative value for **BLOCKQUOTE** elements wouldn't have to be changed to accommodate the difference because the value is based on the previous value.

Percentage Sizes

In addition to using relative sizes like "smaller" and "larger," designers can specify the font size as a percentage of the inherited size. For example, you might want **H1** elements to be 150% the size of regular body text.

```
H1 { font-size: 150% }
```

Length Sizes

Length values specify an exact font size, regardless of the user's settings. The values can be specified as a point, inch, millimeter, or centimeter.

```
H1 { font-size: 24pt }
```

Although length sizes allow the most control over the exact size of text, they are not always the best way to specify the font size because they don't yield scalable designs, or designs that will translate well to different window sizes. Because users browse using varying resolutions and differing browser sizes, it is often better to let the browser control some aspects of your design. Also, as you learned earlier, many visually impaired users will take advantage of the browser's font preferences to specify larger than normal text. Length values will override the user's wishes, often with less than desirable results.

SAVING STEPS: THE FONT PROPERTY

The font property allows designers to control, in one declaration, all other font properties. For example, instead of this list of rules:

```
H1 { font-family: times, serif;
     font-size: x-large;
     font-weight: bold;
     font-variant: small-caps; }
```

you could apply all those values to the font property like this:

```
H1 { font: times, serif, x-large, bold, small-caps; }
```

Obviously, this can make for much simpler code.

text-decoration

The *text-decoration property* allows designers to specify attributes like blinking or underlining to be used.

Available values for the text-decoration property are underline, overline, line-through, and blink. Note that any combination of these values may be included in the declaration. The default value for the text-decoration property is "none."

```
A:link { text-decoration: underline }
```

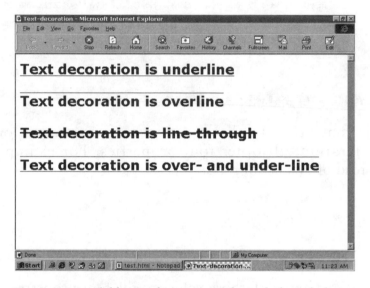

Figure 6.8 *Available text decoration styles include underlining, overlining, line-through, and blink*

When marking up a document for typesetting, a single line under text indicates that it should be set in italics, and a double line indicates that it should be set in uppercase letters. Because of this convention, people started to use underlining to mean the same thing as italics when they italic type wasn't available (with typewriters, for example.) Because underlining can mean the same thing as italic type, use it sparingly.

Additionally, most browsers indicate hyperlinks by underlining the text that is linked. Underlining text that isn't linked can often lead to confused users.

Overline text is used most frequently in science, mathematics, and other specialized applications. It is similar in concept to underlining, except that the line appears above rather than below the text.

Line-through text, often called strikethrough text, is used to denote portions of text that have been (or are to be) removed.

Blinking text is similar to Netscape's `<BLINK>` tag, which causes text to blink incessantly. This, considered to be Netscape's most annoying feature, is rarely used by professional designers. The blink text decoration will probably suffer the same fate of disuse.

An interesting issue with the text-decoration property is inheritance. Although this property has the appearance of being inherited, strictly speaking it is not. Text decorations are actually just "passed through" to their children. This is similar in concept to the way background elements are not inherited, but simply shown through the transparent backgrounds of their child objects. The distinction here is so subtle that most users will never run across an example that illustrates the point, but be aware that such a distinction exists.

Text decoration is not inherited because the designers knew that, although none of the current properties of this attribute would have problems, there is a possibility of problems with future specifications. For more information, visit http://www.internet-nexus.com/css/inherit_tt/.

text-transform

Before CSS, the only way to change the case of text was to retype it. In other words, if a passage was in all lowercase letters, you couldn't make it uppercase without re-keying the entire passage. CSS, however, has a *text-transform property* to solve this problem.

Let's say, for instance, that you want the first letter each word in your headlines to be capitalized. You could declare this using CSS:

```
H1 { text-transform: capitalize }
>...
<H1> i want capital letters </H1>
```

With CSS, that headline might display like this:

I Want Capital Letters

Three values are available in the text-transform property: uppercase, lowercase, and capitalize. The default value is "none."

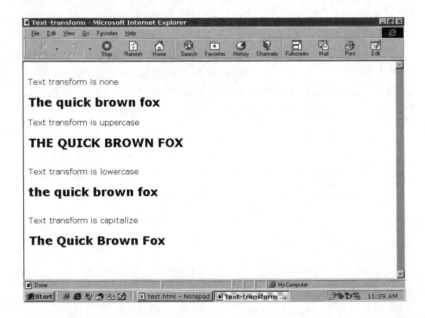

Figure 6.9 You transform text in various ways

Uppercase changes all letters, no matter what their case, to uppercase letters. Lowercase displays all letters in lowercase, and capitalize displays the first letter of each word in uppercase, whereas the rest of the word is lowercase—useful for titles and headlines. Unfortunately, capitalize does not take into consideration standard conventions for capitalizing headlines and titles. (Normally, in English, words like *the* and *of* are not capitalized unless they are the first word in the headline or title.) CSS does, however, take into account language-dependent characters. For example, in French, accent characters are not used in uppercase.

 It is conceivable that companies such as Microsoft and Netscape might see fit to make the capitalize functionality work the way it should, but in current versions they work as outlined in the CSS specification with no enhancement.

REAL-WORLD FONTS

In the real world, you have to deal with using only those fonts that the user is likely to have on his or her machine. How can you guess what users scattered across the globe will have installed? Included here is cheat sheet for sure fire font choices every time.

SLAM DUNK: SURE FIRE FONT CHOICES

The safest font choices you can make are the fonts that ship with common operating systems such as Windows and MacOS. Because the two operating systems ship with different fonts, you will have to choose an alternate value for each platform and list them in order in the font-family property.

 Not all browsers support multiple font choices in the font-family property. This is something that will probably not be a permanent situation, but beware, and as always, test carefully in as many platform/browser configurations as you can!

Cross-Platform

Most sites are targeted at users of both Windows and the Mac. The best thing to do is to provide two font choices, that way you are safe either way. Here are some great font equivalents to use:

- Arial/Helvetica
- Times New Roman/Times
- Courier New/Courier

Windows

The following fonts shipped with Windows 3.1 and NT 3.5, as well as Windows 95 and NT 4. These are safe font choices for about 80% of the computing population:

- Arial
- Comic Sans
- Courier New
- Modern
- MS Sans Serif
- Symbol
- Times New Roman
- Wingdings

MacOS

The following fonts ship with MacOS, and therefore are safe bets when developing for an audience expected to consist of mostly Mac users:

- Chicago
- Courier
- Geneva
- Helvetica
- Monaco
- New York
- Palatino
- Symbol
- Times
- Zapf Dingbats

IN THE PAINT: THE NEXT BEST THING

Of course, man cannot live by default fonts alone. Sometimes you might want to take a little risk. The following sections offer some relatively safe bets for a majority of surfers.

Windows 98 Default Fonts

Windows 98, code-named Memphis, will ship in early 1998 and will include these fonts (and probably a few more):

- Baskerville Old Face
- Book Antiqua
- Bookman Old Style
- Century Schoolbook

- Cooper Black
- Copperplate Gothic
- Eras
- Eurostile
- Franklin Gothic
- Garamond
- Gill Sans
- Goudy Old Style
- Impact
- Lucida
- Lucida Sans
- Stencil

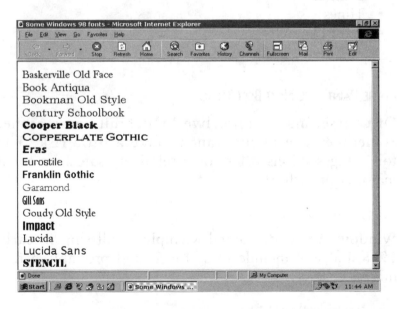

Figure 6.10 *Windows 98 users have access to a wide variety of fonts*

Internet Explorer Fonts

Microsoft's Internet Explorer 3.0 for Windows 95/NT ships with the following fonts:

- Arial Black
- Comic Sans MS
- Impact
- Verdana

Internet Explorer for the Mac ships with a set of fonts that duplicate most of the default Windows set, along with a few extras tagging along for the ride.

- Arial
- Arial Black
- Comic Sans MS
- Courier New
- Georgia
- Impact
- Times New Roman
- Trebuchet

Microsoft's WebFonts

Microsoft has done much to proliferate adequate font support on the Web. In its quest to help out font-hungry Web designers, Microsoft has introduced its freely downloadable WebFont pack. You can grab this pack for free at for both Mac and Windows, so many savvy Web users will have them installed already:

- Arial
- Arial Black
- Comic Sans
- Courier New
- Georgia
- Impact
- Times New Roman
- Trebuchet
- Verdana

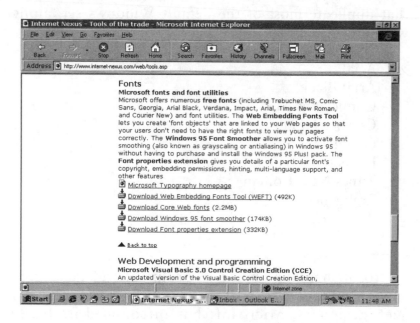

Figure 6.11 *You can download Microsoft's Web fonts from the Internet Nexus Web site (http://www.internet-nexus.com)*

Verdana, by the way, deserves mention as one of the most readable screen fonts available anywhere for font-hungry Web designers—and the price is certainly right!

Microsoft Office Fonts

If ever a suite of applications has reached the point of ubiquity, Microsoft Office is it. Everyone, it seems, has Office. And because Office installs many fonts by default, you can use this to your advantage in your designs. (The following lists only the fonts that are installed on all platforms. Additional fonts are installed in the Windows versions.)

• Arial Narrow
• Arial Rounded Bold
• Book Antiqua
• Bookman Old Style
• Braggadocio
• Brittanic Bold
• Brush Script MT
• Century Gothic
• Colonna MT
• Desdemona
• Footlight MT Light
• Impact
• Kino MT
• Matura MT Script Capitals
• Playbill
• Wide Latin

As you can see, several fonts are listed in more than one category. This just means more chance that users will have them installed, so if you are a bit of a risk taker, go to town!

The Road to No Guessing

The future of CSS involves eliminating the need for guessing. With font embedding technologies like Netscape's dynamic fonts and the initiatives for font downloading in CSS2, you will be able to embed font outlines in your pages, guaranteeing that they will display the same regardless of whether the user has the appropriate fonts installed. The future isn't here yet, but its nice to know that you won't always be stuck trying to second guess the fonts a user is likely to have installed.

CHAPTER 7

Controlling White Space with CSS

Next to the lack of font control, the inadequacy of control over white space in HTML is the biggest gripe for many Web designers. Though CSS helps the situation, it doesn't solve the problem completely. Designers must still rely on tables and sometimes frames for advanced layouts. Most complex designs will use a combination of tables and CSS.

In discussing white space control in CSS, you must again rely heavily on DTP terminology. Don't be concerned if you don't know the difference between kerning and leading, though—everything is explained here.

LEADING AND KERNING

Since the introduction of proportionally spaced fonts, designers have spent a lot of time establishing exactly how much space should exist between each letter and each line of text—called *kerning* and *leading* respectively. These are important facets of design, but were previously unavailable to Web designers. With CSS, some control is finally available.

LEADING WITH THE LINE-HEIGHT PROPERTY

Leading is the amount of space between each line of flowing text. Leading can dramatically affect the visual impact of a design, as well as its readability. As you can see, the two paragraphs in Figure 7.1 look dramatically different, but the only difference is the leading.

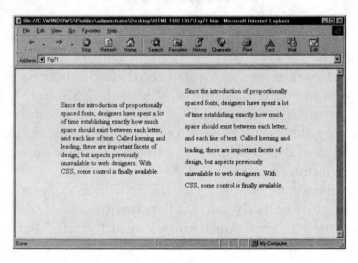

Figure 7.1 Leading can dramatically affect designs.

The paragraph on the left is defined by the following style sheet:

```
P { font-family: Times, Serif;
    font-size: 12pt;
}
```

The paragraph on the right, however, adds the following declaration:

```
line-height: 20pt;
```

The difference is obvious: the lines are spread farther apart. Actually, each line is given more space. Figure 7.2 illustrates this.

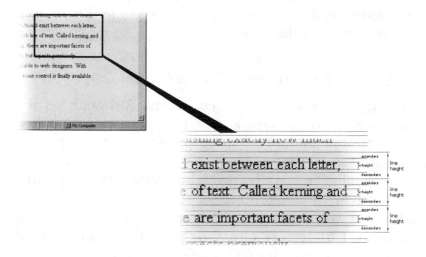

Figure 7.2 The line-height property.

Many aspects go into determining line height: the subtle differences in font styles, the height of ascenders and descenders in the type, and even the width of the text block. Here are a few tips:

- If the lines will be fairly long, consider adding some extra line height to give reader's eyes some extra space to help hold their place in the text.
- Typefaces with unusually long ascenders and descenders can extend the perception of line height,

and the opposite is true of faces with short
descenders and ascenders. You can compensate for
this appropriately with the line-height property.

- Small amounts of text intended to grab the reader's
  attention should have more line height because they
  usually need to be read at a glance.

Like most measurement values in CSS, the line-height
property can have values expressed as a number, length,
or percentage of the type size.

KERNING WITH THE LETTER-SPACING PROPERTY

Kerning is the space between letters. Although setting
this is done by the typeface designer, you can extend or
decrease the amount of space proportionately by using
the *letter-space property.*

Generally, be conservative when setting letter spacing,
moving in small increments to improve readability.
However, when trying to achieve dramatic effects, a wide
dispersal of letters can work wonders when used
sparingly—and almost never in running text. For
example, many designers use wide spacing in logos, such
as the Studio Verso home page displayed in Figure 7.3.

As you can see from the navigational links on the left
side of Figure 7.4, wide letter spacing can be combined
with equally large line height to achieve a dramatic,
ultra-modern feel.

Figure 7.3 Notice the letter spacing in the word Verso.

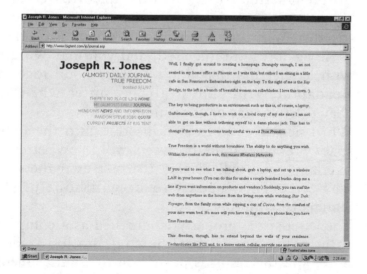

Figure 7.4 Lots of space creates a modern feel.

The CSS code was simple:

```
P { font-family: Verdana, Sans-Serif;
    font-size: 10pt;
    letter-spacing: .5em;
    line-height: 18pt;
  }
```

The letter-spacing property can contain any length value, including points, em units, and even percentages.

Now that you know how to use the letter-space property, you should be aware of a few things to avoid:

- Except in certain circumstances, do not change the letter-space property for running text. Typeface designers spend countless hours specifying how different letter pairs will line up, often creating *ligatures*, or special letter shapes designed to go together. When the letter-space property is changed, these ligatures are not used, and you may wind up with letter pairs that don't look as good together. Readability will almost always suffer when you change letter spacing for running text.
- When negative values are inserted into the letter-space property, some browsers will allow letters to overlap; some will display the text as if the value was zero. This inconsistency will hopefully be eliminated with time.
- The letter-space property is inherited as a computed value. This means that the computation is done once, and the result is passed on to child elements. For example, if the font size of the parent property

is 24 points and you assign the letter spacing to 1em, the computed value of 24 points is passed on to the children regardless of their point size.

Outside the Lines: Space Around Block Elements

Each block element, such as **P** or **H1**, can be imagined to have a box surrounding it as shown in Figure 7.5.

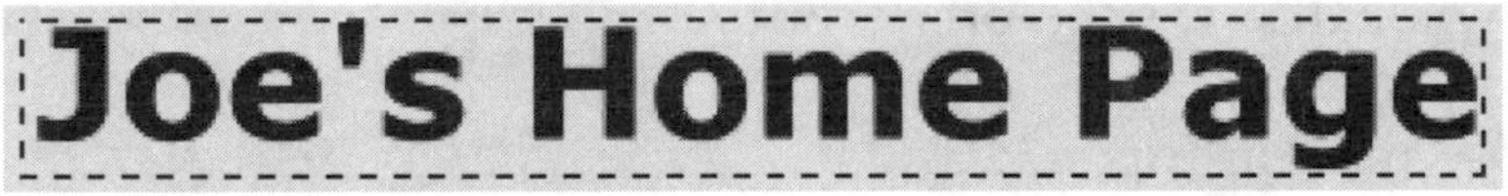

Joe's Home Page

Figure 7.5 Block elements are inside an imaginary box.

Surrounding this box is a series of larger boxes, allowing for space between elements. These boxes are called the *margin*, *padding*, and *border*. These boxes are illustrated in Figure 7.6.

Joe's Home Page
margin
border
padding
element

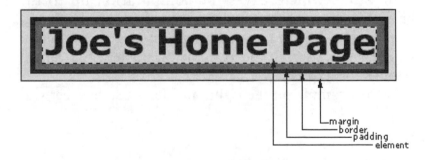

Figure 7.6 The three boxes around block elements.

CSS allows for manipulation of the size of each of these boxes, providing a great deal of control over the spacing in documents.

MARGINS AND PADDING

An element's *margin* is the space between its bounding box. Controlling margins allows the designer to specify the spacing in documents.

There are five margin properties, with the fifth being a "wildcard" for the other four:

- margin-top
- margin-right
- margin-bottom
- margin-left
- margin (sets properties for all four margins at once)

Margins can be set as a width, such as a point value, or as a percentage of the parent object. There is also an *auto* value, which leaves the computation up to the browser, which is the default.

In Figure 7.7, the same paragraph is given different margin properties. In the example on the left, the default settings for Explorer were used.

In the example on the right, a different style sheet was used:

```
P { margin-top: 2in;
    margin-right: 2in;
    margin-bottom: 2in;
    margin-left: 2in;
    }
```

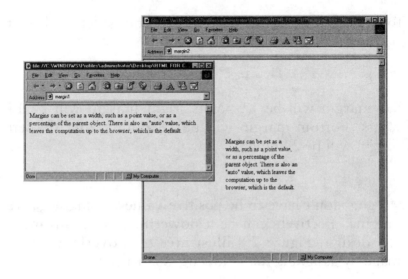

Figure 7.7 Margin control in CSS.

Rather than setting each of the four margins separately, you can assign values in one fell swoop using the margin property. Assigning a single value will set that value to all four properties; or you can specify a pair of values, and the top and bottom will take the first value, and the right and left will take the second. Assigning four values will assign the first value to the top margin, the second value to the right margin, the third value to the bottom margin, and the final value to the left margin.

A few examples follow:

```
P { margin: 12pt }
```

All margins will be 12 points.

```
P { margin: 12pt 24pt }
```

Top and bottom margins will be 12 points; left and right margins will be 24 points.

```
P { margin: 12pt 14pt 18pt 24pt }
```

Top margin will be 12 points, right margin will be 14 points, bottom margin will be 18 points, and the left margin will be 24 points.

Negative Margins

Margins don't have to be positive values. Using negative margins effectively can be a powerful tool in advanced CSS design. Figure 7.8 illustrates text overlapping an image by assigning the following CSS rule:

```
H1 { margin-top: -350px;
    }
```

Figure 7.8 Negative margins at work.

Be careful when using negative margins; some browsers might not support them. At the time of this writing, both Netscape Communicator and Microsoft Internet Explorer offered at least limited support of negative margins, but earlier browsers often have trouble interpreting them and will often substitute a value of zero.

Margins can be used to create pixel accurate layouts in much the same way some WYSIWYG editors allow layout in HTML tables. For an example of pixel-perfect layout using margins, see the case study in Chapter 12.

Collapsing Margins

When dealing with margins, remember that CSS margins are collapsible. This means that when two elements are together instead of adding both margins, the greater of the two is used. For example, let's say that a **BLOCKQUOTE** element with a top margin of 18 points follows a **P** element with only a 12-point bottom margin. Instead of adding the two together for a result of 30 points, the larger 18-point margin of the **BLOCKQUOTE** element will be used, effectively collapsing the margin of the **P** element. Collapsing margins ensure that spacing is consistent throughout a document.

BORDERS

A border can serve to set an element apart from surrounding elements. Previously, the only way to achieve a border around something was to place it in a table, but this is no longer the case. Any element can now be placed within a border.

Controlling borders in CSS is similar to handling margins. There are four independent elements, with a fifth acting as a wildcard:

- border-left
- border-right
- border-top
- border-bottom
- border

There are several properties to deal with when using borders, although each can be contained within the border property:

- border-color
- border-style
- border-width

Border Colors

The *border-color* property sets the color to be used for the border. This color can be defined either as one of the named colors or a numbered RGB value.

 For more information on Web colors, visit Appendix B.

Much like the margin property, colors can be set all at once for the border, or individually for each side.

When one value is set, the while border will be the same color.

When two values are set, the top and bottom of the border will be the first color, and the left and right borders will be the second color.

When four values are set, the colors are applied in the following order: top, right, bottom, and left.

Here are a few examples:

```
BLOCKQUOTE: { border-color: black }
```

The border around the **BLOCKQUOTE** elements will be black.

```
BLOCKQUOTE: { border-color: black red }
```

The top and bottom borders will be black; the left and right borders will be red.

```
BLOCKQUOTE: { border-color: gray black gray black }
```

The top and left borders will be gray, and the bottom and right borders will be black, creating a simple shadow effect illustrated in Figure 7.9.

If a border color is not defined, it will inherit the value of the parent element. For example, if the color of text in a **BLOCKQUOTE** element is black, then black will be assumed as the color of the border unless otherwise specified.

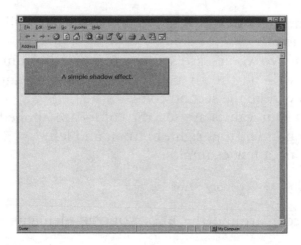

Figure 7.9 A simple shadow effect is created with the border-color property.

BORDER STYLES

Borders don't have to be solid lines, or beveled edges like those of most HTML tables. CSS allows for several different styles of borders, displayed in all their glory in Figure 7.10. The default border style is "none," meaning that no border is drawn.

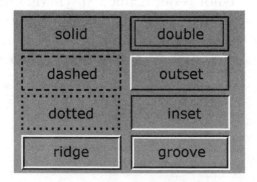

Figure 7.10 CSS border styles.

The following border styles are available in CSS:

- dotted—a dotted line
- dashed—a dashed line
- solid—a solid line
- doublel—two solid lines
- groove—a subtle three-dimensional groove
- ridge—a subtle three-dimensional ridge
- inset—a subtle three-dimensional inset
- outset—a subtle three-dimensional outset

Border styles can be assigned to all four borders independently, or all at once similarly to the border-color property, even the orders are the same.

Setting the Border Width

Border width can be assigned as a constant like a point size, a percentage value, or one of three keywords: *thick*, *medium*, or *thin*. The default value is medium.

The All-In-One Approach: Using the border Property

Fortunately, you can apply all these properties using the all-in-one approach: the border property. This is similar to the way that the font property handles things like font weight and font size.

For example,

```
BLOCKQUOTE { border: solid red thick }
```

would result in the same effect as

```
BLOCKQUOTE { border-style: solid;
             border-color: red;
             border-width: thick;
             }
```

In addition, you can handle the sides of the border separately using the border-top, border-right, border-bottom, and border-left properties.

INSIDE THE LINES: SPACE INSIDE BLOCK ELEMENTS

There are basically two types of internal white space in HTML: *normal* and *preformatted*. In normal blocks, extra white space such as spaces and carriage returns are ignored, whereas in preformatted text all white space is represented on-screen. You can control this using the white-space property. CSS adds a third type of block, called a *nowrap*, in which the text will not wrap at the end of a line.

Examples of the three different block types are illustrated in Figure 7.11.

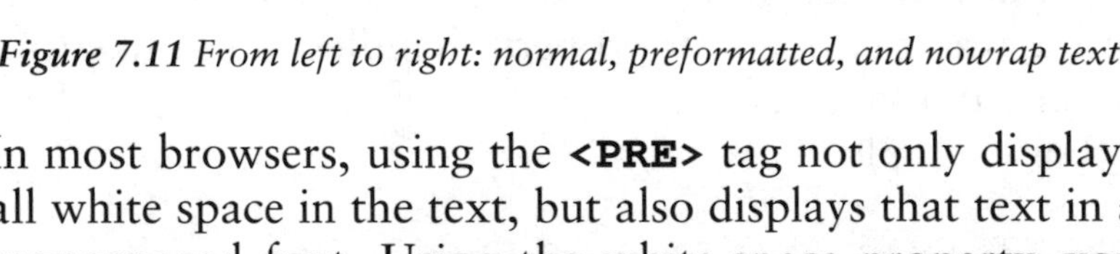

This is a demonstration of a normal text block. Note how the text aligns at the left, but is "ragged" at the right.

```
This is a        demonstration
of a preformatted text block.
   Note that white space is
   preserved in the block.
```

This is nowrap text. No matter what the margins are set as it will not wrap.

Figure 7.11 From left to right: normal, preformatted, and nowrap text.

In most browsers, using the **<PRE>** tag not only displays all white space in the text, but also displays that text in a monospaced font. Using the white-space property, you can finally have preformatted text that displays in a proportionally spaced font.

The examples in Figure 7.11 use the following style sheets.

On the left:

```
P { white-space: normal }
```

In the middle:

```
P { white-space: pre }
```

On the right:

```
P { white-space: nowrap }
```

 Preformatted text will suppress justification, a value to the text-align property, discussed next.

THE TEXT-ALIGN PROPERTY

The majority of text on most Web pages should probably be left-aligned. However, in some cases, you may want to center a block of text, right-align it , or even justify it on both sides.

The following line will align text to the left. This line of code is usually unnecessary because it is the default value, except when you want to specifically override an inherited value:

```
P { text-align: left }
```

This will create centered text, in a way that is similar to the HTML **<CENTER>** tag:

```
P { text-align: center }
```

This will align text to the right:

```
P { text-align: right }
```

The following line will set up the paragraph so that both the left and right margins are even, with the text spread as evenly as possible in between. For an example of justified text see Figure 7.12.

```
P { text-align: justify }
```

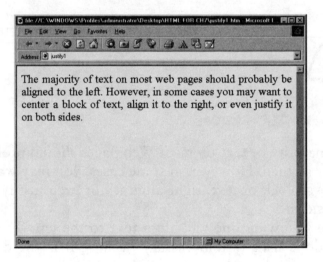

Figure 7.12 Justified text.

Left-aligned text is often called *left justified*, but this is technically incorrect because the word *justified* means to be even at both sides.

SOME NOTES ABOUT JUSTIFIED TEXT

CSS does not specify how justified text is to be handled by the browser. Some browsers will increase the space between individual letters; some will only increase the space between words. Either way, justified text only works well when the lines are fairly long. Figure 7.13 shows the same paragraph justified twice; but the first time, the column is much more narrow. As you can see, the computed space increase between words is much more pronounced in the second example.

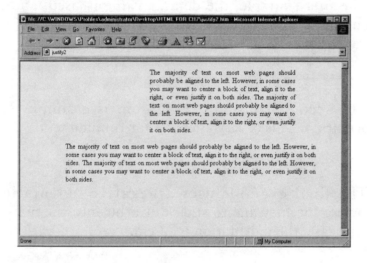

Figure 7.13 Justification is more effective for wider columns.

One way to reduce this tendency would be to hyphenate text, but most browsers do not yet support the separation of words with hyphens.

THE TEXT-INDENT PROPERTY

The text-indent property specifies how much space should be used to indent the first line of a paragraph. This can be specified as either a length or a percentage value.

Indentation is a good way to create a visual cue for paragraph breaks. It is much more subtle and usually more appealing than the usual HTML method of increased white space between paragraphs. Although you can do both, this is usually overkill.

In Figure 7.14, three indentation schemes are used. In the first example, the default value is used, and no visual cue is provided for the beginning of each paragraph.

```
P { text-indent: 0em }
```

The second, and most common, is a simple 2em indentation. This is very effective for running text.

```
P { text-indent: 2em }
```

The final example uses a negative indentation, allowing the first line to stick out a bit into the margin. In this case, the indentation is -2 em.

```
{ text-indent: -2em }
```

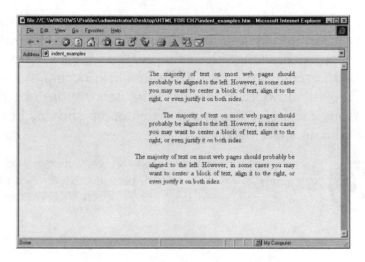

Figure 7.14 Indentation examples.

THE VISIBILITY PROPERTY

The visibility property allows designers to establish the initial display of elements: if an element is defined as *hidden*, it will not be displayed. The primary use of this property is in Dynamic HTML and JavaScript accessible style sheets, both of which are discussed in Chapter 10.

Let's say, for instance, that you want to have an image display only when someone clicks on the correct button for an on-line quiz. You would need to establish that the object should be initially invisible using the following code:

```
IMG.QUIZ { visibility: hidden }
```

When the page is displayed, the image will not be shown, but you can use Dynamic HTML or JavaScript accessible style sheets to change the value of the image's visibility when an event, in this case a button click, occurs.

Keep in mind that *visibility affects layout.* In the previous example, the image will not be shown, but it will take up space on the page.

 Netscape supports the **HIDDEN** value to the visibility property in Windows, but not **VISIBLE**. This is really quite silly because it complicates scripting. Even worse, the Mac version doesnít support the visibility property at all!

IN A PERFECT WORLD: THE FLOAT PROPERTY

The float property is an interesting beast. Using this property, you should be able to accomplish much of what is currently being done with tables: advanced page layout. Unfortunately, browser support is pretty dismal: although Netscape provides limited support, not even the 4.0 version of Explorer supports the float property.

To understand the float property, think of the following HTML:

```
<IMG SRC="someimage.gif" ALIGN="RIGHT">
<P>Here is a paragraph that will wrap around the image:
the image on the right is essentially "floating" to the
right.
```

In the example, the image was "floating" to the right. The same could be accomplished with the following CSS code:

```
IMG { float: right }
```

That code will actually work in all CSS-aware browsers. However, it works only sporadically with elements other than images. This is too bad because it is intended to work with all block-level elements.

The allowed values for the float property are as follows:

- **None:** The default value.
- **Left:** the element is pushed to the leftmost portion of the parent element until it encounters the margin.
- **Right:** the element is pushed to the rightmost portion of the parent element until it encounters the margin.

Margins are mentioned here because some very pleasing effects can be created by subtle manipulations to the margins of floating images.

When using **ALIGN="RIGHT"** in HTML, you would need to use a **<BR CLEAR>** tag to clear out the floatation. In CSS, the clear property is used.

Let's say, for instance, that you have a document where new sections start with **H1** headings. You wouldn't want these headings to wrap around images from the preceding section, so you can add the following code:

```
H1 { clear: both }
```

That code would clear floatation on both the left and the right. Alternatively, you could clear just the left side:

```
H1 { clear: left }
```

Or just the right side:

```
H1 { clear: right }
```

The default value to the clear property is "none," which allows the element to wrap around all floating images.

LAYOUT GROWS UP: CSS POSITIONING

Although not yet an official part of the CSS specification, the document "Positioning HTML Elements with Cascading Style Sheets" has relevance far beyond its official status as a "working draft" at the W3C. Why? Because it was coauthored by browser giants Microsoft and Netscape in an unusual act of cooperation.

Although the draft was in preliminary stages at the time of this writing, there is enough within the draft to give developers a good idea of the power the spec will have. Also, it enjoys support in both 4.0 browsers.

The basics of the "Positioning" draft are simple: using a simple X-Y coordinate system, the position property allows designers to specify the *exact* placement of elements within the browser. As you will see, this is a powerful capability.

THE POSITION PROPERTY

The *position* property allows both relative and absolute positioning of elements within an HTML page using the X-Y coordinate system discussed earlier. An example of X-Y coordinates is displayed in Figure 7.15. This allows elements to be placed *exactly* where the designer intended, whether in relation to the browser or another element. This is, as you can imagine, a good thing.

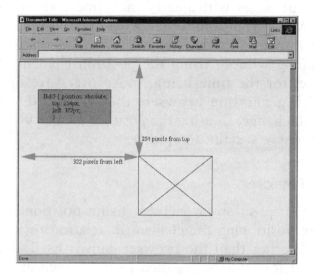

Figure 7.15 The X-Y coordinate system.

ABSOLUTE POSITIONING

Absolute positioning provides a mechanism for establishing an imaginary box around an object and placing that box independently anywhere on the page using the left and top properties.

Here is an example of absolute positioning:

```
IMG.CIRCLE { position: absolute;
             left: 100px;
             top: 200px;
```

In this example, an image has been placed exactly 100 pixels from the leftmost point in the browser's canvas and 200 pixels from the top of the canvas. Any element can be assigned position information, allowing designers to lay out pages with nearly the same level of control they are used to in traditional desktop publishing!

In Chapter 12, you will see an example of CSS positioning without using the position element. This is because, for the time being, more users are browsing with 3.0 generation browsers than with 4.0 versions. This will change, so using the position property will soon become more socially acceptable.

RELATIVE POSITIONING

When you position an element using **position: relative**, you are positioning the element in relation to its parent element rather than the browser canvas itself. This can be useful for layouts designed to work well at multiple resolutions. With the exception of this relationship, relative positioning is handled much the same as absolute positioning.

 Although Navigator 4.0 provides full support for relative positioning, Explorer 4 seems to be conspicuously absent in support of this feature.

CONCLUSION

Now that you understand the basics of CSS, you are ready for more advanced aspects of the spec. This includes complex layout using CSS, scripting with CSS using Dynamic HTML and JavaScript-enhanced style sheets, and even understanding the subtle differences between Netscape and Explorer's support of the CSS specification. The next part of the book focuses on these issues.

PART III:
ADVANCED STYLE SHEETS

CHAPTER 8

Advanced Style Sheets

One of the most exciting aspects of CSS for many Web developers is the capability to create visually interesting sites without resorting to high-bandwidth graphics. Many effects traditionally handled through graphical elements can now be easily approximated with CSS at a fraction of the download size. For example, the two Web pages presented in Figure 8.1 are nearly identical, but the total download time at 14.4Kbps of the one on the right is a few seconds, whereas the screen on the left could take as much as a minute because the effect is achieved by using a single graphical element.

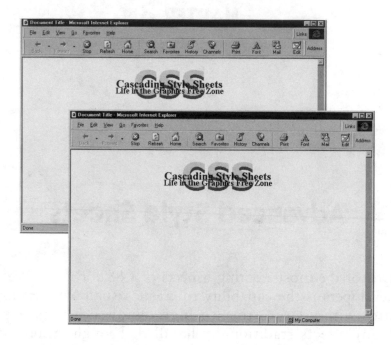

Figure 8.1 Download times can be dramatically improved with CSS: you can't tell the image from CSS.

LIFE IN THE GRAPHICS-FREE ZONE

Obviously, CSS cannot completely replace the use of graphics. It can, however, be used in many instances where graphics have traditionally been used to achieve certain typographical effects. The text overlay effect presented in Figure 8.1, for instance, would have been impossible to achieve without an inline image before CSS, but with a few simple CSS declarations, the effect is relatively easy to duplicate using text. The HTML, for instance, is completely standard:

```
<HTML>
    <HEAD>
        <TITLE>Look ma, no graphics!</TITLE>
    </HEAD>
    <BODY>
        <H1>CSS</H1>
        <H2>
                Cascading
                Style
                Sheets
        </H2>
        <P>
                <A HREF="http://www.w3.org/">Cascading Style
                Sheets</A> allow precise control over white
                space and fonts, but that's not all... by
                manipulating certain properties designers can
                create complex effects previously achieved
                using <A HREF="./images.htm">inline
                images</A>. This contributes to speedy
                downloads and happier users.
        </P>
    </BODY>
</HTML>
```

Adding a couple quick CSS declarations gives the page its layout:

```
BODY { BGCOLOR: White;
       COLOR: Black; }
```

and defines the background color as white, and all **BODY** elements as black.

```
H1 { font: italic 220pt Georgia, Serif;
     color: #dfdfdf ;
     text-align: center; }
```

The **H1** element will act as a "watermark," rendered in a light color that will contrast slightly with the white background.

```
H2 { font: 24pt Verdana, Sans-Serif;
     color: maroon;
     text-align: center;
      margin-top: -2.25in; }
```

Notice that the margin-top property is set to a negative value. This allows it to lay over the "watermark." By using negative margins, designers can place objects over one another, allowing text effects like those shown in Figure 8.2.

```
P { font: 12pt "Times New Roman", Serif;
    text-align: justify;
    line-height: 24pt;
    margin-left: 3.5in;
    margin-right: .75in; }
```

The body paragraph is now made to have wider margins than the rest of the content, making for a narrow column of text. The text has been justified, and the line height, or leading, increased for visual impact.

```
A { color: red;
    text-decoration: none; }
```

This final rule defines the color of hyperlinks, as well as eliminating hyperlink underlining.

ADDING APPEAL WITH LAYERED TEXT

If you want to create a list of sections on your home page you might create a style sheet like this:

```
P { font: Italic 36pt Georgia, Serif;
    font-weight: bold;
    color: C0C0C0; }
```

```
DIV { font: 18pt Verdana, Sans-Serif;
      margin-left: .5in;
      margin-top: -.35in;
      color: #000000;
       margin-right: 5in; }
```

And place HTML like this in a navigational frame:
```
<P>Text
     <DIV>tightly control typefaces and fonts</DIV>
<P>Space
     <DIV>css adds white space control</DIV>
<P>Layout
     <DIV>css can help layout your sites</DIV>
```

The effect can be seen in Figure 8.2.

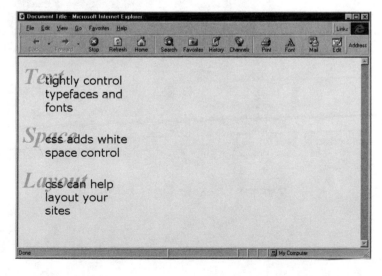

Figure 8.2 Adding visual interest with layered text.

One popular design trick is to apply a *drop shadow* to text. This use to be done by rendering the text as an image, but CSS offers a limited alternative. Figure 8.3 illustrates some text with drop shadows created as both graphics and as CSS rules.

Figure 8.3 Drop shadows in CSS.

To create a drop shadow for text in CSS, all you have to do is render the text twice, in different colors, with a slight offset. Here are two example rules:

```
.shadow { color: black;
          margin-left: 10px;
          margin-top: 10px;
          font-size: 50pt;
          font-weight: bold;
          font-family: Georgia; }
.main   { color: white;
          margin-left: 5px;
          margin-top: -100px;
          font-size: 50pt;
          font-weight: bold;
          font-family: Georgia; }
```

When used with the following HTML a drop shadow like the one displayed in Figure 8.3 is created.

```
<H1 CLASS="shadow">Shadows in CSS</H1>
<H1 CLASS="main">Shadows in CSS</H1>
```

A limitation to this CSS effect is the lack of control over the "focus" of the shadow. When drop shadows are added as images, the shadow element is often dropped out of focus and made transparent like Figure 8.4. Although CSS currently does not provide a mechanism by which this can be accomplished, this feature is expected to appear in a future version of the spec.

Sidebars and quote boxes can also be given limited drop shadows in CSS by using the **BORDER** property because there are constructs for setting for the bottom, left, and right borders.

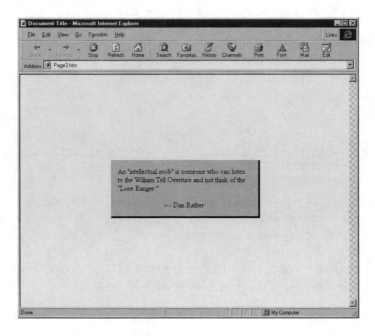

Figure 8.4 Using the BORDER property to create shadows.

```
BLOCKQUOTE { border-bottom: solid;
            border-right: solid;
            background: #C0C0C0;
            padding: 12pt;
            margin: 2in; }
```

By adding a solid border for the right and bottom of the **BLOCKQUOTE** element, a simple drop shadow is created. Although not quite as effective as the best image-based shadows, this is a quick and easy way to get some of the same effect.

ADVANCED CSS EXAMPLES

The four examples shown in Figures 8.5. through 8.8 come from a variety of designers from throughout the web community. Each showcases creativity, good design, and advanced use of at least some CSS features.

Full HTML and style sheet code, as well as links to the example sites themselves, are available on the Web site at http://www.internetnexus.com//web.asp.

EXAMPLE 1: VERDANA

Designer: Simon Daniels

URL: *http:/www.microsoft.com/typography/css/ gallery/slide2.html*

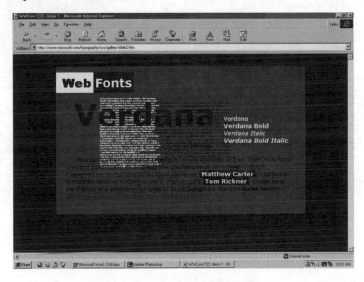

Figure 8.5 Verdana.

Designed by Simon Daniels, this page represents one of the most striking designs yet created in CSS. With extensive use of negative margins and font control, this page is a great example of how CSS helps create visually stunning designs with few or no graphical elements.

EXAMPLE 2: GROW UP

Designer: Simon Daniels
    URL: *http://www.microsoft.com/truetype/css/gallery/4e.htm*

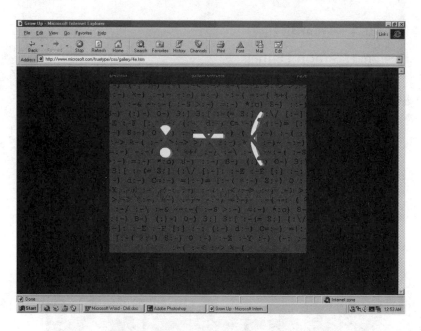

Figure 8.6 Grow Up.

Another Simon Daniels creation, this page uses layered text and subtle color shifts to create a fantastic watermarking effect with the background.

EXAMPLE 3: *WIPED* MAGAZINE

Designer: Joseph R. Jones
    URL: *http://www.internet-nexus.com/web/design.asp*

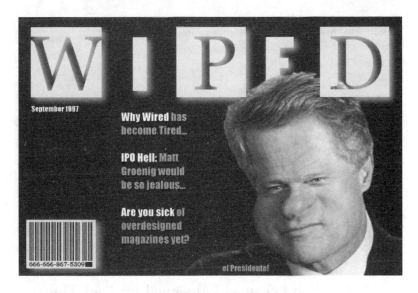

Figure 8.7 Wiped magazine.

Created by Joseph R. Jones, *Wiped* magazine was designed as a parody of Wired magazine's unconventional style. Because of the advanced layout requirements of spoofing such complex design, CSS was used throughout. For an in-depth look at this site, check out Chapter 12.

EXAMPLE 4: INTERNET NEXUS CHANNEL

Designer: Paul Thurrott

URL: *http://www.internet-nexus.com*

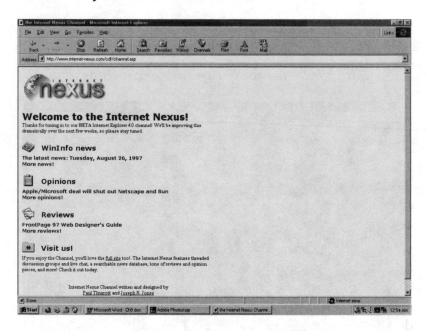

Figure 8.8 Internet Nexus channel.

This IE 4.0 Web "channel," designed by Paul Thurrott, takes advantage of Dynamic HTML and style sheets to increase interactivity, personalization, and design consistency. Because it was designed as an Internet Explorer 4.0 channel, browser support was not an issue, allowing much more flexibility in the CSS implementation.

CHAPTER 9

Reality vs. Theory: CSS Browser Support

The CSS specification is a powerful tool for designers who want more control over information presentation on the Web. However, the success of CSS is in the hands of Microsoft and Netscape because only features supported in their browsers will see widespread use by developers.

The good news is that Microsoft's Internet Explorer 3.0 and newer versions support CSS, as do Netscape's Communicator 4.0 and above. The bad news is that neither offers full support for the spec, and both are going in different directions in terms of extending CSS.

THE FIRST TO MARKET: MICROSOFT INTERNET EXPLORER

Microsoft Internet Explorer 3.0 was the first major browser to support CSS. However, this support was limited, and browsers designed specifically for Explorer's

3.0's CSS parsing engine would not always display correctly in the newer browsers. Most of these issues have been corrected with the release of Explorer 4.0, but at the time of this writing, the majority of Internet Explorer users were using the 3.0 version of the browser rather than the newer, improved 4.0 browser.

When Internet Explorer 4.0 was in early private beta testing, a member of the Explorer development team posted a message to Microsoft's private beta newsgroup outlining some of the changes between the 3.0 and 4.0 CSS implementations. Here is the meat of that message, straight from the horse's mouth:

a)   IE3 did not correctly implement line-height according to the final CSS specification (the specification was approved long after IE3 shipped). IE4 follows the specification to the letter.

b)   IE3 did not implement vertical margin collapsing, as described by the CSS specification, and also inserted non-overridable margins between paragraph elements. IE4 collapses vertical margins together, as per the specification, and vertical paragraph margins are overridden by any top- and bottom-margins on the paragraphs.

c)   IE3 made any style properties coming from stylesheets anywhere in the document structure override any non-stylesheet rendering properties (e.g., if you set text-decoration to "none" for the HTML tag, tags would not be underlined). IE4 applies stylesheet properties in the same manner as HTML properties, so inheritance is the key factor. For example, if you want to remove the underlining on tags, you MUST set "text-decoration: none" on all tags, not on the tag.

d)   IE4 does not yet implement the background image positioning and tiling control.

e)   IE4 DOES, however, implement a number of properties that IE3 didn't - such as font-variant, letter-spacing, overline text-decoration, text-transform, border properties (for the BODY element, IMG elements, and TABLEs and table cells), as well as implementing a considerable portion of the CSS Positioning draft.

f)   IE4 also supports multiple stylesheets, including multiple linked stylesheets, and does not have problems with background images and body properties set through linked stylesheets.

Internet Explorer 4.0 (Figure 9.1) represents arguably the best CSS support currently available in a major browser. It is important, though, that you maintain a realistic perspective on current browser statistics. At the time of this writing, Explorer 4.0 represented less than 10 percent of the hits on most major Web sites.

Figure 9.1 *Internet Explorer 4.0 follows the CSS specification more closely than any other browser.*

GAINING GROUND: NETSCAPE COMMUNICATOR 4.0

Netscape finally brought CSS into the mix with the 4.0 version of its Navigator browser, which is part of the Communicator suite. Communicator's CSS support was unreliable in the early beta versions, but suddenly, in a late beta unveiled weeks before the final release of the product, the stars aligned and Netscape had gotten it right. Communicator's CSS support is now excellent, although still not quite on par with Internet Explorer 4.0.

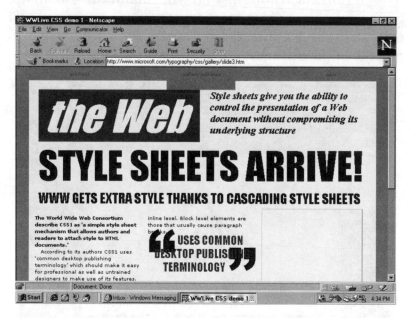

Figure 9.2 Netscape Navigator/Communicator 4.0 finally supports CSS.

Most of Netscape's CSS glitches revolve around font support. For instance, Oblique fonts, small caps, and overline text is not supported in Communicator 4.0. Netscape's staff, however, has been very forthcoming about these deficiencies and promises to remedy most if not all of them in the next Communicator release.

For a complete list of known issues with Netscape's CSS support, visit Netscape's DevEdge Web site at http://developer.netscape.com/.

OUT OF THE LOOP: OLDER BROWSERS

The biggest problem with using CSS in its current infant stage of development is not the spotty support by the new crop of browsers, but rather the complete lack of support by older browsers. Netscape's Navigator 3.0, for instance, supports none of the CSS spec, and at the time of this writing commanded as much as 50 percent of Web users' desktops. Users are looking at the world through Netscape 3.0-colored glasses, and the world they see is one devoid of the advantages of CSS. There are only a couple of things developers can do to combat this unfortunate situation, and none of them is pretty.

DOUBLE DUTY: CREATING TWO SITES

A common tactic employed by early Web developers blazing a trail wrought with the browser-dependent tags and non-standard HTML constructs that ran rampant in the early Web industry was to create separate sites for the "Netscape impaired" viewers. This worked well but was certainly more work. This is much less common now because the vast majority of users has either Netscape or Explorer, both functionally similar products in terms of HTML support.

However, with CSS comes a return of the dual-site strategy. Spawned as much by next-generation development tools as by CSS, this strategy no longer has to take twice as much work.

How can a developer create two versions of a site without manually coding two versions of every page? Simple: by creating dynamic, database driven content that can be easily repurposed for delivery to any browser.

In the early days, Web database integration was a daunting task; but with new tools such as Microsoft's Visual InterDev/ASP technology and Apple's recently acquired Next Web Objects, it is surprisingly easy to do. Although the particulars of deployment are beyond the scope of this book, a look at the concepts behind this new trend towards a more dynamic Web is worth the effort.

For more information on Microsoft Visual InterDev and Active Server Pages technology, visit http://www.microsoft.com/vinterdeu.

For more information about Next Software's Web Objects, visit http://www.apple.com.

In dynamic Web sites, the content itself is in a database, instead of being hard-coded into the site's HTML. This is useful for reasons other than managing multiple versions of the same information: updates are easier because they can be handled through filling out forms rather than directly manipulating source code.

After the information is in a database, programs can be written to get the content out of the database and onto the Web site. Although conventional tools such as

Perl scripts written to the CGI interface can handle this kind of work, more advanced tools such as ASP and WebObjects provide a simpler way to handle this type of programming. With simple SQL calls to the database content embedded in HTML code, the actual creation of pages only needs to occur once by passing arguments to the server through query strings or POST action forms. On the Hip Mama Web site, for example, multiple articles are viewed from the same URL but with a different query string. The server compares the query string to ID numbers of articles in the database and dynamically creates

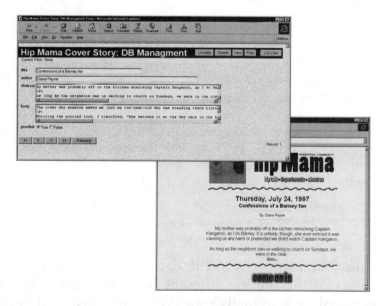

Figure 9.3 The Hip Mama Web Site http://www.hipmama.com/ is managed through HTML forms.

an HTML page with the content from the article that matches. This code is designed for Active Server Pages, but code for other development environments would be functionally similar. (ASP code is contained within `<%` … `%>` delimiters.)

```
<% RequestedID = Request.QueryString("ID") %>
<% Set GirlDBConn =
        Server.CreateObject("ADODB.Connection")
      GirlDBConn.Open "HipMama_DataSource"
      MyQuery = "SELECT ID, title, subtitle, body FROM
      Girl_Mom WHERE (`ID` LIKE [RequestedID])"
    Set QueryResults = GirlDBConn.Execute(MyQuery)
%>
<TABLE BORDER="0" WIDTH="600">
   <TR>
      <TD WIDTH="80">
      </TD>
      <TD>
         <IMG SRC="./gfx/headers/girlmom.gif">
<!--#INCLUDE FILE="nav.asp"-->
         <P>
         <IMG SRC="images/squiggle2.gif"
            WIDTH=551
            HEIGHT=19
            BORDER=0>
         <H2><%= QueryResults("title") %></H2>
         <%= QueryResults("subtitle") %><BR>
         <%= QueryResults("body") %>
```

Because the content is in the database creating separate versions of the site for different browsers, creating two sites is only a marginally time-consuming task and never needs to be updated directly!

Figure 9.4 The results of the Hip Mama ASP code.

Hybrid Web Design: Using Style Sheets in Non-CSS Designs

Another way to take advantage of CSS without abandoning the millions of Web users not yet using browsers that support the spec is to create sites that work without CSS and then add the style sheets to the pages. This strategy, called *Hybrid Web Design*, works well because the site seen by non-CSS browsers was designed from the beginning with the limitations of plain HTML in mind. This strategy does, however, limit how much CSS functionality you can build into your site because the document structure in the HTML files will not be as complete as it would be in a pure CSS design.

For example, consider the example of Hybrid Web Design shown in Figure 9.5. It takes advantage of certain aspects of the CSS specification, such as font control and leading, but is not reliant on the execution of the CSS rules. The page will display well in browsers that don't support CSS. This type of page is said to *degrade* well. In fact, the table that controls the margins and columns is designed in such a way that it will display well in browsers that don't handle HTML tables!

Figure 9.5 Hybrid Web page displayed in CSS and non-CSS browsers.

The code for the page displayed in Figure 9.5 is quite simple, although the nested tables needed for margins and columns make the code seem deceptively complex.

```
<TABLE BORDER="0">
    <TR>
        <TD WIDTH="100">
             
        </TD>
        <TD>
            <FONT SIZE="5" FACE="Verdana,Ariel,Helvetica">
                <H1>Hybrid Web Design</H1>
            </FONT>
            <TABLE BORDER="0" CELLPADDING="32">
                <TR>
                    <TD WIDTH="250" VALIGN="TOP">
                        <FONT SIZE="2" FACE="Times">
                        Content for Column 1
                        </FONT>
                    </TD>
                    <TD WIDTH="250" VALIGN="TOP">
                        <FONT SIZE="2" FACE="Times">
                        Content for Column 2
                        </FONT>
                    </TD>
                </TR>
            </TABLE>
        </TD>
    </TR>
</TABLE>
```

When you are satisfied with the way the page is displaying in non-CSS browsers, you can create a style sheet to be used with the file. The style sheet used with this page is included here:

```
BODY { background: WHITE;
       color: #1F1F1F; }
H1 { color: #0F015B;
     font-family: 36pt Verdana, sans-serif;
     font-weight: bold; }
P { font-family: 12pt Times, Serif;
    line-height: 1.5;
    text-align: justify;}
EM { background: yellow }
```

With Hybrid Web Design, you can create complex, aesthetically pleasing designs that degrade well in older browsers a win-win situation.

TECHNOLOGY TO THE RESCUE: BROWSER-SENSING

Now for the whiz-bang, way cool, bleeding edge approach: you can sense what browser a visitor to your Web site is using and send appropriate content to her based on that information. This can be done using Microsoft's Active Server Pages technology built into its Internet Information Server or using a conventional CGI program. The problem with this approach is that, one way or another, you still have to develop two versions of the site, either separate files or through "if then else" statements in the code. Although time-consuming, the end result is often well worth the effort.

A browser-sensing CGI is easy to write because all it really has to do is look at the environment variables passed to the server from the user's browser to figure out what program is being used and send the user to an appropriate page. For example:

```
If ($ENV{'HTTP_USER_AGENT '} eq "Mozilla" {
   Print "Location: netscape.html \n\n";
   }
else {
      Print "Location: other.html \n\n";
      }
```

Although the preceding example, written in Perl, is overly simplified, it shows how such a program would be written. The same function, written in VBScript for ASP would look like this:

```
<% If Request.ServerVariables("HTTP_USER_AGENT ") =
"Mozilla" Then
      Response.Redirect "netscape.html"
   Else
      Response.Redirect "other.html"
   End If
%>
```

 Active Server Pages actually includes a server component that provides information about the capabilities of the user's browser.

By providing multiple versions of your site and detecting browsers, you can provide a user experience tailored to the browser in a manner that is transparent to the end user. That way, you can take full advantage of CSS with no compromise in favor of backward compatibility.

CHAPTER 10

Style Sheets and Scripting

Although Cascading Style Sheets do create a level of control over the layout and design of your Web pages that was unheard of with plain HTML, the current CSS specification does little to address the dynamic nature of the Web itself. People have come to expect Web sites that resemble multimedia CD-ROMs more than print publications, and to duplicate that sort of interactivity, you're going to need access to some programmatic capabilities. For example, you might want to change the style of a block of text as the mouse moves over or clicks it. Or you might want to play a sound. As you might imagine, the possibilities are limitless.

Both Microsoft and Netscape have recently solved the problem of merging the CSS specification with these and other dynamic capabilities. Unfortunately, they did so in two totally different ways. There are some similarities, however. Both Microsoft and Netscape realized that to create a sort of *dynamic style sheet*, they would need to marry two existing Web technologies: CSS and Web scripting. This chapter explores these solutions and points out the likely path that the W3C will follow in ratifying them as a Web standard. First, though, let's take a quick look at what we mean by *Web scripting* so that you can see how developers created dynamic sites before CSS entered the picture.

OVERVIEW OF WEB SCRIPTING

When HTML was first created, the point was to create a simple mark-up language that could describe the general look of text in a document. Programs that could interpret this mark-up, now known as *Web browsers*, provided only the most basic of document displays. As the Web became more pervasive, however, companies such as Netscape and Microsoft enhanced the HTML language with proprietary tags in an attempt to provide their users with a richer experience. One of the most successful additions was that of scripting languages. A *scripting language* allows the Web developer to program content in Web pages. With a scripting language, Web pages can be dynamic rather than static. You can use a scripting language to respond to user choices, display confirmation dialog boxes, and perform other tasks previously available only to application programmers.

Unlike true programming languages, however, scripting languages are *interpreted*, meaning that they run line by line as the page loads. Most scripting code is parsed in the same way as HTML code. In fact, scripting code and HTML code can be intertwined in a Web document in the same way that CSS can be intertwined with HTML code.

Though there are some other possibilities, the two most popular Web scripting languages by far are JavaScript and VBScript. The following sections take a look at these languages and discusses their relative benefits.

Scripting languages such as JavaScript and VBScript are worthy of entire books. Although we will try to provide a usable overview here, we cannot do these topics the justice they deserve in this single chapter. Understanding Web scripting languages is imperative if you want to use them with style sheets, so you may want to invest some time with other scripting references as well. Check out the Internet Nexus Web scripting site for more information: http://www.internet-nexus.com/web/scripting.asp.

JAVASCRIPT

JavaScript began its life as LiveScript and was created by Netscape Corporation for its Navigator 2.0 Web browser. Around the same time, Sun's Java language began to take off, so Netscape, sensing a market opportunity, changed the name of LiveScript to JavaScript. This confused the public: most people are probably unaware that JavaScript and Java are two totally different technologies and have little, if anything, to do with each other.

JavaScript was designed from the ground up as a Web scripting language, but it resembles arcane programming languages such as C and C++, making it difficult to learn for all but the most technical people. The following

JavaScript code demonstrates how you can use the language
to detect the browser that is currently viewing your page:

```
<SCRIPT LANGUAGE="JavaScript">
<!--
strVar = navigator.appVersion + '<BR>'

if (navigator.appName == "Microsoft Internet Explorer")
{
  if (strVar.substring(0,1) == "4")
    document.write("You are using MSIE 4")
  else
    if (strVar.substring(0,1) == "3")
      document.write("You are using MSIE 3");
}
else {
  if (navigator.appName == "Netscape")
  {
    if (strVar.substring(0,1) == "4")
      document.write("You are using Netscape 4")
    else
      if (strVar.substring(0,1) == "3")
        document.write("You are using Netscape 3");
  }
}
// -->
</SCRIPT>
```

There are a couple of things to note here. First, Web
scripting code is generally enclosed in a **<SCRIPT>**
block, similar to the way CSS is enclosed in a **<STYLE>**
block. The HTML comment lines (**<!--** and **// -->**)
ensure that older browsers to do not try to display the
scripting code. Because this example uses JavaScript
code, the initial **<SCRIPT>** tag includes a **LANGUAGE**

attribute that is set to "JAVASCRIPT". As for the language itself, you can see that it is pretty ugly. All it does is print out the name of the browser you are using, assuming that it is one of the browsers it checks for.

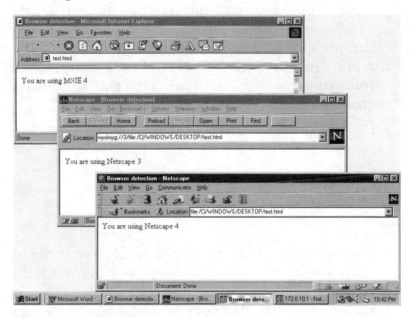

Figure 10.1 The JavaScript browser detection code running on three different Web browsers.

If you're uncomfortable with programming languages, JavaScript is not going to make you a convert. To really harness the power of JavaScript, you have to learn some pretty serious programming skills. JavaScript does have one overwhelming benefit, however: more than 90% of browsers currently in use support JavaScript. Netscape Navigator 2, 3, and 4 support it, as does Internet Explorer 3 and 4.

Typically, JavaScript is used for the following purposes:

- **To programmatically control the appearance and content of the current document.** You can use the JavaScript *write* method (see the preceding code sample) to output any text—including HTML code—to the Web browser. For example, the following code has the same effect as if you had created the **<H1>** block in HTML:

```
<SCRIPT LANGUAGE="JavaScript">
<!--
document.write("<H1>This was created with
JavaScript</H1>");
// -->
</SCRIPT>
```

- **To control the browser itself.** JavaScript provides the capability to control the behavior of the browser, get information about the browser (as in the browser detection code above), or even to open a new browser window. For example, the following will open a new Web browser window when the page containing this code is viewed (Figure 10.2):

```
<SCRIPT LANGUAGE="JavaScript">
<!--

Features = "toolbar=no, status=no, menubar=no,
resizable=no, "
Features = Features + "scrollbars=yes, width=640,
height=480"
```

```
window.open("http://www.internet-
nexus.com/main.asp"'
"wndNexus",
            Features);
// -->
</SCRIPT>
```

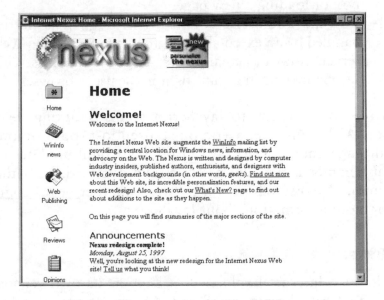

Figure 10.2 *This browser window was created with JavaScript code.*

- **To control the document's content.** JavaScript lets you interact with the current HTML document. For example, you can programmatically access all the hyperlinks, forms, and form elements in the document.
- **To interact with the user.** Many developers use JavaScript to perform form verification before a

form is sent to the Web browser. If a particular field isn't filled out, JavaScript can open a dialog box telling the user that the form must be completed before it is sent. You can also handle *events* with JavaScript. For example, if the user clicks a button, you can handle that "event" by opening a dialog box or loading a new page.

- **To read and write cookies.** Although it is better handled by an executable program running on the Web server, you can actually read and write cookies with JavaScript code that runs right in the user's browser.

If this introduction to JavaScript seems daunting, fear not. Although it is a complex, pseudo-programming language, much of the JavaScript code you'll use later in this chapter is actually pretty straightforward. Visit the Internet Nexus Web site (http://www.internet-nexus.com) for more information about JavaScript.

VBSCRIPT

Although Internet Explorer does support its own version of JavaScript known as *JScript*, Microsoft really wants developers to use its own scripting language, known as *Visual Basic Scripting Edition*, or *VBScript* for short. VBScript is a member of the Visual Basic family, which currently consists of the following:

- **Visual Basic 5.0:** Visual Basic is a full-featured object-oriented programming language capable of creating application programs that run in the Windows 95/NT environments. It also supports the creation of ActiveX controls.

- **Visual Basic 5.0 Control Creation Edition (CCE):** This special version of Visual Basic allows you to create ActiveX controls that can be used in Microsoft's Internet Explorer Web browsers. It is available free from Microsoft. Visit http://www.microsoft.com/vbasic for details.
- **Visual Basic for Applications 5.0 (VBA):** VBA is the macro language used to control almost all of Microsoft's Office 97 applications and a host of other applications from a variety of manufacturers.
- **VBScript:** Microsoft designed a fast, lightweight version of Visual Basic that can be used in Web pages.

All Visual Basic languages look and feel the same, so if you're proficient in VBScript, you'll have no problem picking up one of the other languages. Because the Visual Basic language is so simple, most people who know HTML can learn it quite easily. For example, the following VBScript code displays the phrase "Hello, world!" several times at different sizes, as shown in Figure 10.3:

```
<SCRIPT LANGUAGE="VBSCRIPT">
<!--
   For Size = 1 to 6
      Document.write "<FONT SIZE=" & Size & ">"
      Document.write "<BR>Hello, world!</FONT>"
   Next
-->
</SCRIPT>
```

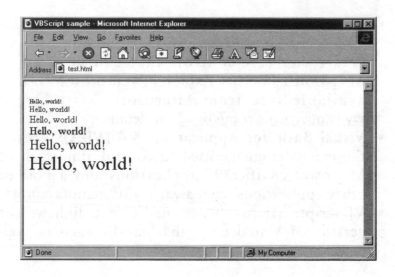

Figure 10.3 *You can mix VBScript and HTML code for interesting effects.*

Note that VBScript and HTML code are easily mixed. VBScript is a simple language that resembles HTML, so the two fit well together. As for features, VBScript can do basically everything that JavaScript can do, and it's much easier to work with.

VBScript has one problem, however; it is only supported on Microsoft Internet Explorer 3.0 and 4.0 at this time. Netscape has pledged to support VBScript in the future, but at this writing, there is no evidence of that.

Using VBScript, then, is not an obvious choice: if you want your sites to run correctly in both Netscape and IE, then JavaScript is your only realistic scripting choice at this time. This is unfortunate on many levels because JavaScript *is* difficult to learn. We'll try to stay away from too much complex JavaScript code in the coming pages, but we are forced to use JavaScript rather than VBScript if only to ensure compatibility with the greatest number of users.

USING OBJECTS

You may have heard the term *object-oriented* before. Both VBScript and JavaScript are pseudo-object-oriented scripting languages, meaning that they programmatically support a group of *objects*. To scripting languages, an object is the browser window or something inside the window, such as the current document, the current location, or a form in the current document. Like CSS, these objects are assembled in a hierarchy, and they support various attributes. For objects and scripting languages, these attributes are known as *properties*. For example, the document object has a *bgColor* property. The *bgColor* property, which corresponds to the HTML **BGCOLOR** attribute of the **<BODY>** tag, determines the background color of the document. You can set properties in JavaScript like so:

```
<SCRIPT LANGUAGE="JavaScript">
<!--
  document.bgColor = "RED";
// -->
</SCRIPT>
```

Objects also support *methods*, which are things the object can do. For example, the document object has a *write* method that writes text to the current document. The following code writes a simple message to the current document:

```
<SCRIPT LANGUAGE="JavaScript">
<!--
  document.write("This text is written in the current")
  document.write(" font to the document.")
// -->
</SCRIPT>
```

Finally, objects can respond to *events*. An event is something that happens to an object. You respond to an event with an event handler, which is a section of code that executes in response to a particular event. For example, the following code changes the background color of a document to yellow when the mouse moves over the hyperlink. The event, in this case, is MouseOver, so the event handler is OnMouseOver.

```
<A HREF="test.html" OnMouseOver='document.bgColor =
"#FFFFCC"'>Go to text</A>
```

Notice that the code is created inline, right inside the **<A>** tag. Doing so is common practice with JavaScript, but you could also call a separate function. A *function* is simply a block of code with a name. You run the function by calling its name in JavaScript code. The following is some scripting code using a function that duplicates the preceding example:

```
<A HREF="test.html" OnMouseOver='doit()'>Go to text</A>

<SCRIPT LANGUAGE="JavaScript">
<!--
  function doit() {
    document.bgColor = "#FFFFCC"
  }
//-->
</SCRIPT>
```

DYNAMIC STYLE SHEETS

Given this brief overview of scripting languages, you may be wondering whether this technology could somehow be mated to style sheets. If you could match the programmability of scripting with the visual appeal of style sheets, for example, your Web site could take on a whole new persona.

Microsoft and Netscape agree, but they each took slightly different approaches to solving the problem. With the release of their version 4.0 Web browsers—Microsoft Internet Explorer 4.0 and Netscape Navigator 4.0—the two companies have indeed combined the elegance of style sheets with the power of scripting. Let's take a look at what they did.

THE MICROSOFT SOLUTION

Microsoft has developed an extension to the existing scripting interface that works with both VBScript and JavaScript called *Dynamic HTML*. Microsoft's implementation of Dynamic HTML allows Web developers to dynamically update the content, style, and structure of an HTML document at any time, giving developers control over the appearance, interactivity, and multimedia elements they want to use.

The object model in Dynamic HTML is designed so that styles can be changed on-the-fly. In the current CSS specification, you can apply styles to various elements before the page loads; then those styles remain static until a new page is loaded. Using Dynamic HTML, you can change styles at any time.

Dynamic HTML is more than just styles, however. This new technology also gives you access to every object in the document, not just the objects used in the scripting object model. This means that every bit of text, graphic, Java applet, or whatever appears in your Web page can be modified on-the-fly with Dynamic HTML.

THE NETSCAPE SOLUTION

Netscape, for its part, has also developed an extension to HTML, which, unfortunately, is also called dynamic HTML. For purposes of this book, we will be referring to Netscape's technology as *dynamic HTML* (with a small *d*) for reasons explained in the next section.

Netscape's dynamic HTML allows you to change styles on-the-fly, just as Microsoft's Dynamic HTML does. Netscape accomplishes this in a different way than Microsoft, however, and it only works with JavaScript. Additionally, Netscape Dynamic HTML provides a downloadable font capability (so that users can easily get the fonts you're using) and a 2D positioning system. These capabilities are also present in Internet Explorer 4.0.

W3C AND THE FUTURE OF DYNAMIC SCRIPTING

If we seem harsh towards Netscape, there's a reason: Microsoft developed its version of Dynamic HTML with the W3C, collaborating on the feature set so that it could easily be ratified as an official Web standard in the future. Netscape, however, went its own way and developed competing technology that will not likely become a standard. The problem with Netscape's approach is that most of its technology simply duplicates work the W3C has done, but in a nonstandard, incompatible way. For a company that pays so much lip service to open standards, Netscape has done as much as it can to drive standards to its own ends.

For these reasons, we will focus on Dynamic HTML as envisioned by Microsoft because that is the likely route the W3C will follow as it standardizes future versions of HTML and creates an official Document Object Model (DOM). Because Netscape has pledged to support these standards, it is likely that Netscape will eventually adopt this technology as well.

However, we will provide a short overview of Netscape's dynamic HTML at the end of this chapter

INTERNET EXPLORER 4.0 DYNAMIC HTML

Dynamic HTML consists of the following features:

- **Dynamic styles:** The styles used to display text can change at any time, even continuously.
- **Dynamic positioning:** Objects in a Web page can be positioned dynamically in 2D space, with z-ordering, at any time.
- **Dynamic content:** You can actually change the contents of a page after it has finished loading.
- **Event bubbling:** An object can handle an event (such as MouseOver) or pass it along to a parent object.

As you might gather from the preceding list, the thing we're most interested in here is dynamic styles. Let's take a look.

DYNAMIC STYLES

Cascading Style Sheets gives Web developers control over the look and feel of HTML elements, but *dynamic styles* take it to the next level. Dynamic styles provide the capability to dynamically change *any* attribute, at any time, of *any* HTML element in a Web page.

The best part is that no new HTML tags were needed to accomplish this.

Consider the following simple DHTML example:

```
<H1 onclick="this.style.color = 'Navy';">Click me till
I'm blue!</H1>
```

When this heading one text is clicked, its color changes to navy blue. You can provide the same type of effect with images, as well. In the following code, the image changes when the mouse pointer moves over it:

```
<IMG SRC="before.gif" onmouseover="this.src =
'after.gif';">
```

Both these samples use the *this* object, which is simply a way to ensure that any style changes you make apply to the current object. This is convenient because it allows you to skip naming the elements. Of course, you could also explicitly name the element with the **ID** attribute. The following code duplicates the functionality of the first DHTML example but provides an explicit name for the **H1** tag:

```
<H1 ID="MyH1" onclick="MyH1.style.color = 'Navy';">Click
me till I'm blue!</H1>
```

MAKING YOUR DOCUMENT DYNAMIC

In the previous examples, the changes didn't require the layout to change: all you did was change the color of some text. With Dynamic HTML, however, it is possible to change any attribute of any element, so you could actually change the size of the text as well, and the document would not have to reload. Microsoft calls this feature *reflow*, which it compares to *reload*. When you reload a page, the document flashes, and the entire page actually reloads from the Web. With Dynamic HTML, you can change a style dynamically, and the affected element—and the elements around it—will reflow to accommodate the change. Let's see what this looks like.

The following HTML document has three sections of text, one of which is surrounded by a **SPAN** block. Normally, the **SPAN** block allows you to add an inline style, but with Dynamic HTML, you can also use it to identify a block of text and then handle the event that occurs when the mouse moves over it.

```
<HTML>
<BODY BGCOLOR="#FFFFFF">
Here is some text. Blah blah blah blah blah blah.
<SPAN STYLE="color: blue"
  onclick="this.style.fontSize = '36pt'">
Click this text!
</SPAN>
Here is some more text. Blah blah blah blah blah blah.
</BODY>
</HTML>
```

Figure 10.4 shows what this page will look like before you interact with it. Figure 10.5 shows the results of having clicked on the text in the **SPAN** block. The size of the text changes instantly to 36-point, and the text around it flows naturally.

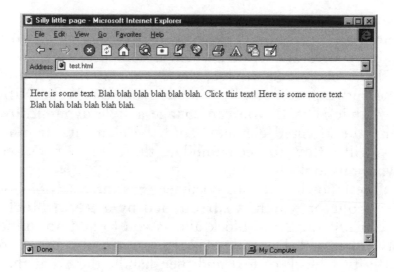

Figure 10.4 A silly little page before a mouse-click.

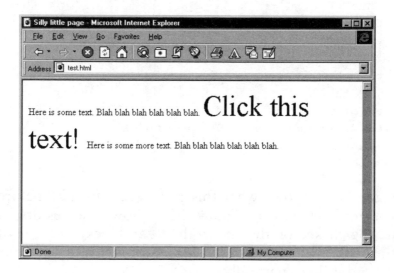

Figure 10.5 And after.

One problem with this code is that the mouse cursor doesn't change into the famous pointing hand that users associate with hyperlinks. Dynamic HTML gives you the new *cursor* attribute to do this. The following code simulates a hyperlink:

```
<SPAN STYLE="cursor: hand; color: blue; fontsize=12pt"
onclick="this.style.fontSize = '36pt'">
Click this text!
</SPAN>
```

This allows you to provide your users with a visual cue that clicking an element will *do* something. When you use standard HTML hyperlinks, it's obvious to the user that clicking the link will change the document in some way. Because DHTML allows such fine control over every element in the page, however, it's nice to be able to let your users know which elements will do something and which will not.

HIDING AND SHOWING TEXT

Dynamic HTML also provides ways to hide an element, such as some text, and then redisplay it. This can be done in two ways: You can make text simply disappear, or you can make the text disappear and have the elements below that text reflow into the space previously occupied by the text. When you make the text reappear in this second case, the text then reflows properly below the text again.

Let's look at the first case. To make text disappear and reappear, you can use the new CSS *visibility* attribute. The visibility attribute can be set to *visible* or *hidden*. If an element is visible, you will see it in the document. If it is hidden, you will not see it. At first glance, it may seem that this attribute is faking its effect, perhaps by setting the color of the text to the background color when you set it to hidden. This is not the case, however. When you set the visibility attribute of an element to hidden, it literally disappears. If a graphic or other text is behind that element, it will show through as if the element you hid was never there. Here's some code that will alternatively hide and show a text element when you click on a **H1** above it:

```
<HTML>

<BODY BGCOLOR="#FFFFFF">
<H1 STYLE="cursor: hand"
 onclick="ToggleVisibility(ToggleText);">
 Click Me!</H2>
<SPAN ID=ToggleText>I become invisible</SPAN>
<BR>More text.
</BODY>

<SCRIPT>
function ToggleVisibility(e) {
  if (e.style.visibility == "hidden") {
    e.style.visibility = "visible";
  } else {
    e.style.visibility = "hidden";
  }
}
</SCRIPT>

</HTML>
```

When you load this document, you'll see the simple Web page shown in Figure 10.6. Clicking the H1 text will cause the text below it to disappear, as shown in Figure 10.7. Note that the text below it doesn't reflow to occupy the space previously used by the hidden text.

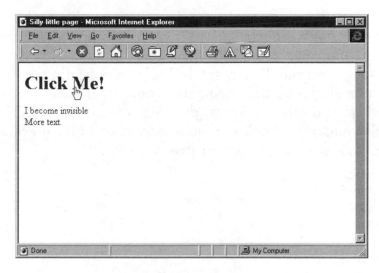

Figure 10.6 The H1 text in this example can be clicked...

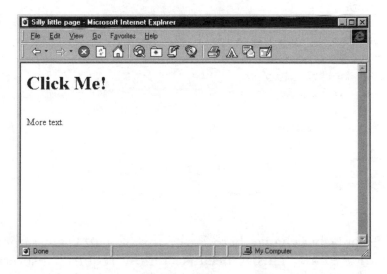

Figure 10.7 ...causing the text below it to disappear.

The next step is to use extent this example to cause the text below the span to reflow and occupy the space previously used by the now-hidden text. Changing the visibility attribute isn't enough, so Dynamic HTML provides a new *display* attribute too. The display attribute has two possible values, *none* and *""* (empty). If display is none, the element is not displayed, and elements around that element will reflow. If display is empty, the element is displayed. The following code sample is a modified version of the previous example using display rather than visibility:

```
<HTML>

<BODY BGCOLOR="#FFFFFF">
<H1 STYLE="cursor: hand"
 onclick="toggleDisplay(DisplayToggle);">
 Click Me</H1>
<DIV ID=DisplayToggle>I go away</DIV>
More text more text more text more text more text
</BODY>

<SCRIPT>
function toggleDisplay(e) {
   if (e.style.display == "none") {
      e.style.display = "";
   } else {
      e.style.display = "none";
   }
}
</SCRIPT>

</HTML>
```

The only big change here is the use of a **DIV** tag rather than a **SPAN**. This is because reflow requires discrete blocks of text to work properly. Figure 10.8 shows the familiar page, but when the heading is clicked, the second line of text disappears, and the text below that reflows to occupy that space. This is shown in Figure 10.9.

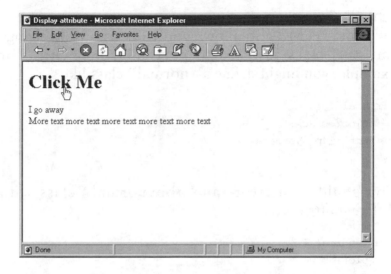

Figure 10.8 The H1 text in this example can also be clicked...

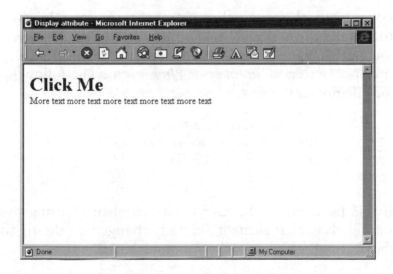

Figure 10.9 ...causing the text below it to disappear and the other text to reflow to occupy that space.

Fun with Classes

Dynamic HTML also allows you to dynamically change the style class assigned to particular elements. For example, you might define a "normal" class like so:

```
.normal {
  color: black;
  font: 14pt Verdana
}
```

You could then create an "abbynormal" class with different attributes:

```
.abbynormal {
  color: blue;
  font: 48pt Comic Sans MS
}
```

You could then use these classes in your HTML document normally. With Dynamic HTML, however, you can change the class of an element dynamically, say in response to a *mouseover* or *click* event. The following code demonstrates this:

```
<DIV STYLE="cursor: hand" CLASS="normal"
  onclick="this.className = 'abbynormal'">
Click me and I just won't be myself!
</DIV>
```

In this page, when the user clicks an element using the normal class, that element's class is changed on-the-fly to abbynormal. This is shown in Figure 10.10.

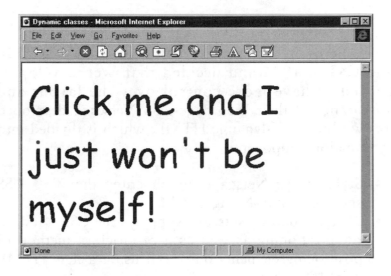

Figure 10.10 *Clicking a perfectly normal element does this!*

WHERE TO GO FROM HERE

Dynamic HTML deserves more space than we can give it here. If you want to look into the other features of this technology more closely, we recommend the following Web pages:

Dynamic HTML (Microsoft) http://www.microsoft.com/workshop/author/dhtml/

Internet Explorer 4.0 home page (Microsoft) http://www.microsoft.com/ie/

NETSCAPE COMMUNICATOR "DYNAMIC" HTML

Like Microsoft, Netscape looked at the state of HTML and CSS in 1996 and decided that Web developers needed to have more control over the layout and appearance of their Web pages. So Netscape developed its own brand of dynamic HTML, which is divided into three major components:

- **Style sheets:** Netscape implemented the W3C CSS specification in Navigator 4.0.
- **2D positioning:** Netscape supports the CSS standard for positioning as well as a proprietary method of positioning elements on-screen using a new HTML `<LAYER>` tag.
- **Downloadable fonts:** A method to use specific fonts and ensure that your users will see your pages correctly.

Netscape also added a method of accessing style attributes from JavaScript. This technology is known, simply enough, as *JavaScript style sheets*.

You may wonder why you'd want to bother with JavaScript style sheets (JSS) if Netscape supports the standard CSS-type styles. Well, JSS is Netscape's way of providing programmatic styles similar to the features explored earlier for Internet Explorer 4.0. Using JSS, you can dynamically change element styles after the page has loaded. Of course, your users will need to be using Navigator 4.0 for this feature to work.

WHERE TO GO FROM HERE

A discussion of Netscape's dynamic HTML also deserves more space than we can give it here. If you want to look into the other features of this technology more closely, we recommend the following Web pages:

Dynamic HTML in Netscape Communicator (Netscape)http://developer.netscape.com/library/documentation/communicator/dynhtml/index.htm
DevEdge Online (Netscape)
http://developer.netscape.com/index.html

PART IV:
GOOD DESIGN: WEB SITES WITH STYLE

CHAPTER 11

Case Study: Basic Style Use

Big Tent Media Labs, a Bay Area interactive publishing company, uses CSS as a way to maintain consistency on its Web site. Because much of the content on the site is dynamic and many people are involved in maintaining the site's content, Big Tent decided it would be easiest to keep the content as close to basic HTML as possible and handle all presentational aspects using CSS. This is a simple application of CSS, so a line-by-line explanation of the source code is unnecessary.

BIG TENT, BIG TABLES

 Big Tent's home page address is http://www.bigtent.com/.

The first thing you notice when you visit the site, shown in Figure 11.1, is the table-based layout. The design is actually a series of nested tables, but it never gets so complex that it becomes difficult to maintain.

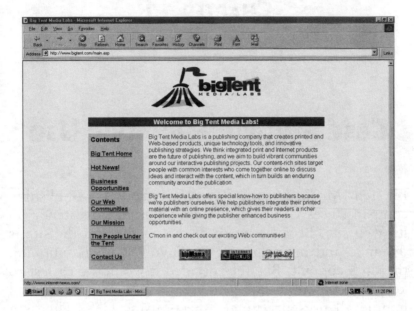

Figure 11.1 Big Tent's home page.

The full HTML for the page is included below:

```
<html>
    <head>
        <title>Big Tent Media Labs</title>
        <LINK REL="STYLESHEET" HREF="./bt.css">
    </head>
    <body bgcolor="#FFFFFF"
          text="#000000"
          link="#000099"
          vlink="#000099">
        <table border="0"
               cellpadding="0"
               cellspacing="0"
               width="650">
            <tr>
                <td align="center" width="100%">
```

```
            <img src="images/newtentwide.gif"
               width="310"
               height="117">
            <br>
            <img src="images/spacer.gif"
               width="10"
               height="15">
         </td>
      </tr>
      <tr>
         <td align="center"
            width="100%"
            bgcolor="#663399">
            <H1>Welcome to Big Tent Media
               Labs!</H1>
         </td>
      </tr>
      <tr>
         <td align="center" width="100%">
            <img src="images/spacer.gif"
               width="10"
               height="15">
         </td>
      </tr>
   </table>
   <table border="0"
         cellpadding="0"
         cellspacing="0"
         width="650"
         cols="3">
      <tr>
         <td valign="top" width="150">
            <table border="0"
               cellpadding="6"
               cellspacing="0"
               width="100%"
```

```
                    bgcolor="#CCCCFF">
            <tr>
                    <td valign="top">
<H2>Contents</H2>
<P CLASS="toc">
<A HREF="main.asp">Big Tent Home</A>
<P CLASS="toc">
<A HREF="news.asp">Hot News!</A>
<P CLASS="toc">
<A HREF="bizops.asp">Business Opportunities</A
<P CLASS="toc">
<A HREF="communities.asp">Our Web Communities </A>
<P CLASS="toc">
<A HREF="mission.asp">Our Mission</A>
 <P CLASS="toc">
<A HREF="us.asp">The People Under the Tent</A>
<P CLASS="toc">
<A HREF="feedback.asp">Contact Us</A
<BR>
<IMG SRC="images/spacer.gif" WIDTH=10 HEIGHT=15>
</b></td>
                    </tr>
            </table>
            </td>
        <td valign="top" width="15"> </td>
        <td valign="top" width="485">

        <P>Big Tent Media Labs is a publishing
            company that creates printed and
            Web-based products, unique
            technology tools, and innovative
            publishing strategies. We think
            integrated print and Internet
            products are the future of
            publishing, and we aim to build
            vibrant communities around our
```

interactive publishing
projects. Our content-rich sites
target people with common interests
who come together online to discuss
ideas and interact with the
content, which in turn builds an
enduring community around the
publication.
<P>Big Tent Media Labs offers
special
know-how to publishers because
we're publishers ourselves. We
help
publishers integrate their printed
material with an online presence,
which gives their readers a richer
experience while giving the
publisher enhanced business
opportunities.
<P>C'mon in and check out our
exciting
Web communities!
<P>
<CENTER>
<TABLE WIDTH=300
     COLS=3
     BORDER=0
     CELLPADDING=5
     CELLSPACING=5>
  <TR>
    <TD WIDTH=100
        ALIGN=CENTER
        VALIGN=MIDDLE>
      <A
HREF="http://www.hipmama.com"><IMG

```
SRC="images/button_hipmama.gif" WIDTH=88 HEIGHT=31
BORDER=0></A>
                    </TD>
                    <TD WIDTH=100
                        ALIGN=CENTER
                        VALIGN=MIDDLE>
                        <A
HREF="http://www.internet-nexus.com"><IMG
SRC="images/button_nexus.gif" WIDTH=88 HEIGHT=31
BORDER=0></A>
                    </TD>
                    <TD WIDTH=100
                        ALIGN=CENTER
                        VALIGN=MIDDLE>
                        <A
HREF="http://www.lofy.com">
<IMG SRC="images/button_lofy.gif"
WIDTH=88 HEIGHT=31 BORDER=0></A>
                    </TD>
                </TR>
            </TABLE>
            </CENTER>
            <br><br><br>
            <DIV CLASS="copyright">
            Copyright ©1997 Big Tent Media Labs
        <BR>
          <a href="mailto:thurrott@bigtent.com">
          Webmaster@bigtent.com
          </DIV>
        <P>
            <DIV CLASS="bestie">
            Best experienced with
        <BR>
          <a href="http://
          www.microsoft.com/ie/default.asp">
            <img src="images/ie_animated.gif"
```

```
                                   alt="Microsoft Internet
                                   Explorer"
                                   border="0"
                                   vspace="3"
                                   width="88"
                                   height="31"></A>
                        <BR>
                            <a href="http://www.microsoft.com/
                            ie/default.asp">
                            Click here to start.</A>
                        </DIV>
                            </td>
                    </tr>
                </table>
        </body>
</html>
```

The style sheet for the site is as follows:

```
H1 { font: 18pt bold Verdana, Sans-Serif;
     color: white;
     margin-bottom: 5pt;
     margin-top: 5pt;
     }
H2 { font: 14pt bold Verdana, Sans-Serif;
     color: black;
     margin-bottom: 3pt;
     margin-top: 3pt;
     }
P.toc { font: 14pt bold Verdana, Sans-Serif;
        color: white;
        margin-bottom: 15pt;
        margin-top: 15pt;
        }
.copyright { font: 9pt bold Verdana, Sans-Serif;
        color: black;
```

```
      margin-bottom: 2pt;
      margin-top: 2pt;
      text-align: center;
      }
.bestie { font: 9pt bold Verdana, Sans-Serif;
         color: black;
         margin-bottom: 2pt;
         margin-top: 2pt;
            text-align: center;
         }
P { font: 12pt bold "Times New Roman", Serif;
         color: black;
         margin-bottom: 10pt;
         margin-top: 10pt;
         margin-left: .5in;
         text-align: justified;
         }
```

By using the same style sheet on each page with the LINK element. Big Tent ensures that all pages maintain a consistent look and feel, one of the most basic capabilities of CSS. Although Big Tent's Web site is far from "cutting edge" in terms of CSS technology, it represents a good application of style sheets for an organizational site.

CHAPTER 12

Bleeding Edge Style

Wiped magazine is a parody of the highly unconventional *Wired* magazine. Because *Wiped* is a parody of a magazine with such unusual design, some pretty complex CSS code is needed to make everything work correctly.

COVER PAGE

Like many CSS designs, the HTML for the *Wiped* cover page is extremely simple—the complexity lies in the CSS code. That way, the page displays well in any browser—even text-based browsers such as Lynx. *Wiped* magazine, located at the Internet Nexus (http://www.internet-nexus.com) is shown in Figure 12.1.

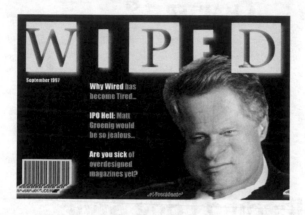

Figure 12.1 Wiped magazineís cover page.

When viewing the HTML, the only tips that there is more than meets the eye are the **LINK** tag referencing the style sheet and the use of **DIV** and **CLASS**.

```
<HTML>
    <HEAD>
        <TITLE>Document Title</TITLE>
        <LINK REL="STYLESHEET" HREF="./css/wiped.css">
    </HEAD>
```

Now that the wiped.css style sheet has been referenced, relatively mundane HTML code will produce the desired results with ease.

```
<BODY BACKGROUND="./images/blueback.gif"
        TEXT="FFFFDD"
        ALINK="FF0000"
        VLINK="FFFFFF"
        LINK="FFFFFF">
```

A standard **BODY** element is used instead of establishing
color schemes in CSS to enhance backward compatibility
with non-CSS browsers.

```
<CENTER>
<TABLE BORDER="0" WIDTH="600">
```

The site is contained within a 600-pixel table so that it
will display the same at all resolutions. As you will see,
this allows exact positioning of elements by
manipulating margins in CSS.

```
<TR>
    <TD>
        <A HREF="toc.asp">
        <IMG SRC="./images/cover.gif"
            ALT="Wiped Magazine"
            BORDER="0"></A>
        <DIV CLASS="month"> September 1997
</DIV>
```

The "month" class will be referenced in the style sheet.

```
<H2> <A HREF="story1.asp">Why Wired</A>
    has become Tired...
<P> <A HREF="story2.asp">IPO Hell:</A>
    Matt Groenig would be so jealous...
<P> <A HREF="story3.asp">Are you sick</A>
    of overdesigned magazines yet?</H2>
<DIV CLASS="tagline"> el Presidente! </DIV>
    </TD>
</TR>
</TABLE>
</BODY>
</HTML>
```

As you can see, the HTML is not only simple, but extremely backward compatible. Now for the CSS code:

```
.month { font: 12pt impact, sans-serif;
         margin-left: 15px;
         margin-top: -305px;
         }
```

The "month" class is placed within the cover graphic right under the "w" in the masthead (see Figure 12.1) by using a negative margin. This allows exact, pixel-level control of layout without resorting to browser-specific code.

```
.tagline { font: 12pt impact, sans-serif;
           margin-left: 315px;
            margin-top: 85px;
           }
```

Again, margins are declared in pixels so that they will be exact in relation to the image and table.

```
H2 { font: 14pt impact, sans-serif;
     margin-left: 120px;
     margin-right: 270px;
     margin-top: 20px;
     line-height: 18pt;
     }
```

Fonts are tightly controlled to achieve the effect.

```
A { text-decoration: none }
```

Hyperlink underlining is disabled to maintain a more print-based look and feel. The color shift should be enough to indicate the links, and if not, the rest of the page is linked to the table of contents.

TABLE OF CONTENTS

The Table of Contents page for *Wiped* magazine, shown in Figure 12.2, has slightly more complex HTML than the cover page. The CSS code is fairly simple.

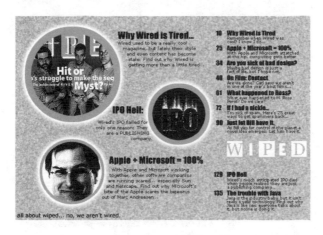

Figure 12.2 Wiped Table of Contents page.

```
<HTML>
    <HEAD>
        <TITLE>Wiped Magazine: Contents</TITLE>
        <LINK REL="STYLESHEET" HREF="./css/toc.css">
    </HEAD>
    <BODY BACKGROUND="./images/toc_back.gif"
        TEXT="000000"
```

```
ALINK="FF0000"
VLINK="555555"
LINK="555555">
```

Again, standard HTML color constructs are used to maintain compatibility.

```
<CENTER>
<TABLE BORDER="0" WIDTH="600">
   <TR>
      <TD VALIGN="top">
         <A HREF="/cgi-bin/toc.map">
      <IMG SRC="./images/tocmap.gif"
            BORDER="0"
            ALT=""
            ISMAP
            ALIGN="LEFT"></A>
      </TD><TD>
```

Note that the table is now two columns.

```
<OL><A HREF="story1.asp">
   <LI>Why Wired is Tired...<BR></A>
      <DIV CLASS="abstract">
      Remember when Wired was cool?
      I know I do...
```

Each TOC item is a list item within an ordered list. That way, pagination is automatic, and the numbers are automatically in the margin.

The "abstract" class will be made into a smaller typeface in the style sheet, but non-CSS browsers will show larger text. This actually works out pretty well.

```
</DIV><A HREF="story2.asp">
            <LI>Apple + Microsoft = 100%</A>
               <DIV CLASS="abstract">
```

```
                  With Apple and Microsoft cooperating
                  at the helm, the computer industry
                  is on more stable ground than ever
          </DIV><A HREF="story3.asp">
              <LI>Are you sick of bad design?</A>
                  <DIV CLASS="abstract">
                  Maybe bad design is a fact of
                  life, but I hope not...
          </DIV><A HREF="story4.asp">
              <LI>On Film: Contact</A>
                  <DIV CLASS="abstract">
                  Are we alone? Carl says "no" in one
                  of the year's best films
          </DIV><A HREF="story5.asp">
              <LI>One Hit Wonders</A>
                  <DIV CLASS="abstract">
                  In the tradition of Ace of Base,
                  Netscape is about to take the "One
                  Hit Wonder" crown
          </DIV><A HREF="story6.asp">
              <LI>If I had a nickel...</A>
                  <DIV CLASS="abstract">
                  I, for one, am sick of spam. Join me
                  in my crusade with the 25 ways to
                  get spammers back
          </DIV><A HREF="story7.asp">
              <LI>Just let him have it...</A>
                  <DIV CLASS="abstract">
                  As Bill Gates vies for control of
                  the world an interesting idea
                  emerges: just let him have it.
          <P>
              <DIV CLASS="masthead">
              Wiped magazine <BR>
              <IMG SRC="./images/masthead.gif"> <BR>
              September 1997<BR>
              </DIV>
```

```
            <P>
            </DIV><A HREF="story8.asp">
            <LI>IPO Hell</A>
                <DIV CLASS="abstract">
                Wired's IPO fell apart when
                everyone realized they are a
                <i>publishing</i> company, not a
                <i>technology</i> company.
            </DIV><A HREF="story9.asp">
                <LI>The trouble with Java...</A>
                <DIV CLASS="abstract">
                Java may be the media sweetheart,
                but it may not be a valid technology.
                See why programming Java is like sex:
                everyone is talking about it, but
                nobody is actually <i>doing</i> it.
            </OL>
            </TD>
        </TR>
        </TABLE>
    </BODY>
</HTML>
```

Now for the CSS code:

```
OL { font: 12pt impact, sans-serif;
    }
.abstract { font: 8pt verdana, sans-serif;
            }
.masthead { font: 9pt verdana, sans-serif;
            }
```

The font is the only thing declared for the each selector:

```
A { text-decoration: none }
```

Again, turning off hyperlink underlining.

AN ARTICLE

By far the most complex pages on the *Wiped* site are the articles because many of them are designed to sit on, and perfectly match up with, complex background images. As you can see in Figure 12.3, this is no easy task.

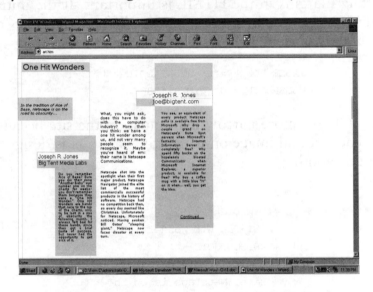

Figure 12.3 The match has to be down to the pixel!

The HTML gets pretty complex because the flow of the content must be in the right order for non-CSS browsers, and even browsers that don't support tables.

```
<HEAD>
    <TITLE>One Hit Wonders -- Wiped
    Magazine</TITLE>
    <LINK REL="STYLESHEET" HREF="./css/story5.css">
```

```
</HEAD>
<BODY BACKGROUND="./images/art_back.gif"
      TEXT="000000"
       ALINK="FF0000"
       VLINK="990000"
       LINK="000099"
       TOPMARGIN="0"
       LEFTMARGIN="0">
```

Setting margins in the HTML is important. If the initial value isn't zero, it becomes more difficult for CSS to accurately place text.

```
<TABLE BORDER="0" CELLPADDING="0"
CELLSPACING="0" WIDTH="580">
```

This table is more narrow than most on the site because the background image on which the page sits is designed for this width.

```
<TR>
    <TD WIDTH="220">
        <H1>One Hit Wonders</H1>
        <BLOCKQUOTE>
        In the tradition of Ace of <BR>
        Base, Netscape is on the <BR>
        road to obscurity...
        </BLOCKQUOTE>
```

Notice that the **BLOCKQUOTE** element contains a brief overview of the article.

```
<H2>Joseph R. Jones<BR>
    Big Tent Media Labs</H2>
```

The author information is in an **H2** element because it will one of the more important aspects of the page.

```
<P CLASS="abstract">
```

The following paragraph isn't really an abstract, but it will be used for indexing the site, so it is labeled as such.

```
Do you remember Ace of Base? Sure you do:
their song "Another Baby" was number one
on the charts for weeks-you don't
remember them because they were a
"One Hit Wonder." One Hit Wonders
are bands that race to the top of
the charts, only to be lost in a
sea of obscurity the following month.
I always felt bad for these bands,
since they got a brief taste of
success, but never had the opportunity
to get sick of it.
</TD><TD>
<P CLASS="first">
```

The initial paragraph is in a slightly different type size so that it stands out as the place for the eye to start. This is important in non-standard layouts such as this.

```
What, you might ask, does this have to
          do with the computer industry? More
          than you think: we have a one hit wonder
          among us, and not very many people seem
          to recognize it. Maybe you've heard of em:
          their name is Netscape Communications.
<P CLASS="main">
```

Most paragraphs will be classified as "main."

```
Netscape shot into the spotlight when
                their first major product, Netscape
                Navigator joined the elite list of the
                most commercially successful products
                in the history of software.
                Netscape had no competition back then,
                so every day seemed like Christmas.
                Unfortunately for Netscape, Microsoft
                noticed. Having awoken Bill Gates'
                "sleeping giant," Netscape now
                faces disaster
                at every turn.
                </TD><TD WIDTH="180">
```

Although the table isn't nested, because of the tight margin control allowed by CSS, the layout will be exact.

```
                <DIV CLASS="author">
                Joseph R. Jones<BR>
                joe@bigtent.com
                </DIV>


                <P CLASS="second">
```

This "second" class will be treated nearly the same as the first.

```
You see, an equivalent of every product Netscape
                sells is available free from Microsoft.
                Why drop a couple grand on Netscape's
                Suite Spot servers when Microsoft's
                fantastic Internet Information
                Server is completely free? Why spend
                fifty bucks on the hopelessly bloated
                Communicator when Microsoft Internet
```

```
Explorer, a superior product,
is available for free? Why buy a coffee
mug with a little blue "N" on it
when... well, you get the idea.

<DIV CLASS="cont">
        <A
HREF="story5_cont.asp">Continued....</A>
        </DIV>

</TD>
        </TR>
      </TABLE>
    </BODY>
</HTML>
```

Now for the style sheet:

```
H1 { font: 18pt "Comic Sans", sans-serif;
     margin-left: 15px;
     margin-top: 10px;
     }
```

There is only one **H1** element, and it is supposed to fit inside a yellow box on the background. To do this, the margins have to be exact.

```
BLOCKQUOTE { font: italic 8pt Verdana, Sans-Serif;
             margin-left: 8px;
             margin-top: 95px;
             line-height: 9pt;
             width: 100px;
             }
```
The BLOCKQUOTE element, too, needs to fit into a small box.
```
H2 { font: 12pt "Comic Sans", sans-serif;
     margin-left: 60px;
```

```
    margin-top: 115px;
    line-height: 14pt;
}
```

The **H2**, you may recall, is for the author's information.

```
.abstract { font: 7pt Verdana, Sans-Serif;
            margin-left: 120px;
            margin-top: 5px;
            line-height: 7pt;
            text-align: justify;
          }
```

The justified text will look better in columns than standard left-aligned text. This is only the case because of the bounding box design. Usually, justified text is more difficult to read.

```
.main { font: 7pt Verdana, Sans-Serif;
        margin-left: 25px;
        margin-top: 20px;
        margin-right: 25;
        text-align: justify;
      }
.first { font: 8pt Verdana, Sans-Serif;
         margin-left: 25px;
         margin-top: 150px;
         margin-right: 20;
         text-align: justify;
       }
.second { font: 7pt Verdana, Sans-Serif;
          margin-left: 25px;
          margin-top: 20px;
          margin-right: 20;
          text-align: justify;
        }
```

```
.author { font: 12pt Verdana, Sans-Serif;
         margin-left: 0px;
          margin-top: 35px;
         margin-right: 25;
         text-align: left;
         line-height: 14pt;
         }
.cont { font: 8pt Verdana, Sans-Serif;
         margin-left: 25px;
          margin-top: 70px;
         margin-right: 25;
         text-align: right;
         }
```

As you can see, the pixel-perfect capabilities of CSS are the only way this design could have happened.

CHAPTER 13

Converting Existing Web Sites to CSS

Cascading Style Sheets are great if you are building a Web site from the ground up, but what if you have an existing Web site that you would like to modify to take advantage of CSS technology? No problem. You might not be able to easily take advantage of all aspects of Style Sheets, but many features are easy to plug into existing HTML.

Adding CSS to an existing Web site is analogous to repainting a house, or knocking it down to bare foundation and building it again from scratch—the depth of your desired changes will dictate how much demolition has to take place.

REPAINTING THE WEB

The most basic CSS retrofit consists largely of grafting some styles and declarations to mostly unmodified HTML code. This isn't always possible for sites that are complex designs, since there may often be very little document structure to attach rules to—you may need to add some "primer."

This primer will take the place of document structure information grafted into your HTML. If you have very basic (almost HTML 2.0 compliant) code this won't be necessary, but the vast majority of sites will require at least a little bit of work in order to accept CSS rules.

Let's say, for example, that you have used the **FONT** element in your HTML rather than conventional **H1** elements for headlines. You will need to add some type of identifying mark that you can easily use as a CSS selector. This is usually done with **DIV** and **SPAN**.

USING DIV AND SPAN

Let's take a look at the home page for Big Tent Media Labs, pictured in Figure 13.1.

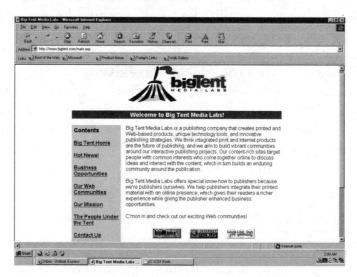

Figure 13.1 The Big Tent Web site before CSS.

```
<body bgcolor="#FFFFFF"
    text="#000000"
    link="#000099"
    vlink="#000099">
<center>
<table border="0" cellpadding="0" cellspacing="0"
width="650">
    <tr>
        <td align="center" width="100%"><img
        src="images/newtentwide.gif" width="310"
        height="117"> <br>
        <img src="images/spacer.gif" width="10"
        height="15"> </td>
    </tr>
    <tr>
        <td align="center" width="100%" bgcolor="#663399"
        height="25">

<font color="#FFFFFF" size="4" face="Arial"><b>Welcome to
Big Tent Media Labs!</b></font></td>
    </tr>
    <tr>
        <td align="center" width="100%"><b><img
        src="images/spacer.gif" width="10" height="15">
</b></td>
    </tr>
</table>
</center>
<table border="0" cellpadding="0" cellspacing="0"
width="650"
cols="3">
    <tr>
        <td valign="top" width="150"><table border="0"
        cellpadding="6" cellspacing="0" width="100%"
        bgcolor="#CCCCFF">
            <tr>
                <td valign="top"><b>
```

```
<FONT FACE="Arial" SIZE=4
COLOR="#000000"><B>Contents</B></FONT>
<P><FONT FACE="Arial" SIZE=3><A HREF="main.asp">Big Tent
Home</A>
<P><A HREF="news.asp">Hot News!</A>
<P><A HREF="bizops.asp">Business Opportunities</A>
<P><A HREF="communities.asp">Our Web Communities </A>
<P><A HREF="mission.asp">Our Mission</A>
<P><A HREF="us.asp">The People Under the Tent</A>
<P><A HREF="feedback.asp">Contact Us</A>
</FONT>
<BR><IMG SRC="images/spacer.gif" WIDTH=10 HEIGHT=15>
</b></td>
            </tr>
        </table>
        </td>
        <td valign="top" width="15"> </td>
        <td valign="top" width="485">
            <font size="3" face="Arial">
<P>Big Tent Media Labs is a publishing company that
creates printed and Web-based products, unique
technology tools, and innovative publishing strategies.
We think integrated print and Internet products are the
future of publishing, and we aim to build vibrant
communities around our interactive publishing projects.
Our content-rich sites target people with common
interests who come together online to discuss ideas and
interact with the content, which in turn builds an
enduring community around the publication.
<P>Big Tent Media Labs offers special know-how to
publishers because we're publishers ourselves. We help
publishers integrate their printed material with an
online presence, which gives their readers a richer
experience while giving the publisher enhanced business
opportunities.
<P>C'mon in and check out our exciting Web communities!
<CENTER>
<TABLE WIDTH=300 COLS=3 BORDER=0 CELLPADDING=5
CELLSPACING=5>
```

```
<TR>
    <TD WIDTH=100 ALIGN=CENTER VALIGN=MIDDLE>
        <A HREF="http://www.hipmama.com"><IMG
SRC="images/button_hipmama.gif" WIDTH=88 HEIGHT=31
BORDER=0></A>
    </TD>
    <TD WIDTH=100 ALIGN=CENTER VALIGN=MIDDLE>
        <A HREF="http://www.internet-
nexus.com"><IMG SRC="images/button_nexus.gif" WIDTH=88
HEIGHT=31 BORDER=0></A>
    </TD>
    <TD WIDTH=100 ALIGN=CENTER VALIGN=MIDDLE>
        <A HREF="http://www.lofy.com"><IMG
SRC="images/button_lofy.gif" WIDTH=88 HEIGHT=31
BORDER=0></A>
    </TD>
    </TR>
</TABLE>
</CENTER>
<br><br><br>
</font>
<CENTER>
<font size="2" face="Arial">Copyright © 1997
Big Tent Media Labs</font><font size="3"
face="Arial"> <br>
</font><a href="mailto:thurrott@bigtent.com"><font
size="3" face="Courier New">Webmaster@
bigtent.com</font></a><font
size="3" face="Arial"> <br>
</font><P><CENTER><font size="1"
face="ARIAL,HELVETICA"><b>Best
experienced with<br>
</b></font><a
href="http://www.microsoft.com/ie/
default.asp"><font
size="1" face="ARIAL,HELVETICA"><b><img
src="images/ie_animated.gif"
```

```
        alt="Microsoft Internet Explorer" border="0"
        vspace="3"
        width="88" height="31"> </b></font></a><font
        size="1"
        face="ARIAL,HELVETICA"><b><br>
        Click here to start.</b></font><font size="3"
        face="Arial"> </font></p>
      </td>
    </tr>
  </table>
</center>
```

This source code, created by Microsoft's FrontPage, is pretty tough to read, and makes heavy use of **FONT** tags instead of structural tags like **H1** and **BLOCKQUOTE**. This is fine, but some information will need to be added to graft CSS Style declarations to this HTML.

First, let's take a look at the "welcome" header at the top of the page. We don't want to remove the **FONT** tag, as this would destroy the effect in non-CSS browsers. We simply want to enclose the welcome in a **<SPAN>** element:

```
<SPAN CLASS="HEADER">
<font color="#FFFFFF" size="4" face="Arial"><b>Welcome
to Big Tent Media Labs!</b></font>
</SPAN>
```

Now, we can add the following declaration to the style sheet:

```
SPAN.HEADER { font-family: Ariel Sans-Serif;
                          font-size: 4;
                          color: black;
              }
```

Next, we can take a look at the navigational text in the sidebar.

Again, we don't want to remove the presentational information here, we simply want to add the same information to the style sheet. In this case, a **DIV** element will be used.

```
<FONT FACE="Arial" SIZE=4
COLOR="#000000"><B>Contents</B></FONT>
<DIV CLASS="NAVIGATION">
<P><FONT FACE="Arial" SIZE=3><A HREF="main.asp">Big Tent
Home</A>
<P><A HREF="news.asp">Hot News!</A>
<P><A HREF="bizops.asp">Business Opportunities</A>
<P><A HREF="communities.asp">Our Web Communities </A>
<P><A HREF="mission.asp">Our Mission</A>
<P><A HREF="us.asp">The People Under the Tent</A>
<P><A HREF="feedback.asp">Contact Us</A>
</DIV>
</FONT>
```

Now, we can apply some CSS rules to the NAVIGATION class, on our style sheet:

```
DIV.NAVIGATION { font-family: ariel sans-serif;
                 font-size: 3;
                 }
```

Finally, we will attack the main paragraph text.

In this case, we will want to actually change the display of text slightly in CSS browsers, taking advantage of a capability that doesn't exist in non-CSS browsers: justified text.

All we need to do is replace the **<P>** tags with **<P CLASS="MAIN">** tags, and apply a set of rules to that class:

```
P.MAIN { font-family: ariel sans-serif;
         font-size: 3;
         text-align: justify;
         }
```

Now that we have mapped styles where nessesarry, we may want to apply a couple of extra global styles to enhance the display of the site in CSS browsers without modifying the HTML code. For example, we could remove hyperlink underlining:

```
A { text-decoration: none }
```

 Sites that have been converted to CSS should link to external style sheets, since manually embedding rules in the HTML defeats the purpose of adding style sheets. To see how to do this, see Chapter 4.

BUILDING A NEW FOUNDATION FOR CSS

Sometimes, a quick paint job isn't enough. Instead, you will want to create new pages that have more structure to them, and take advantage of CSS to mimic the original style of the site.

Again, we will use the Big Tent Web site, but we will start over from scratch this time around, adding much needed structure to the code. You will be amazed how simple the actual HTML will be this time around!

```
<IMG SRC=" images/newtentwide.gif" WIDTH="310"
HEIGHT="117">
<H1> Welcome to BigTent Media Labs! </H1>
```

The welcome message is simply placed into an **H1** element. Using CSS we can simply provide a background color for the text, duplicating the look and feel of the old site without nearly as much code.

```
<TABLE BORDER="0" CELLPADDING="5">
  <TR>
    <TD WIDTH="33%" BGCOLOR="#CCCCFF ">
      <DIV CLASS="NAVIGATION">
      <P><A HREF="news.asp">Hot News!</A>
      <P><A HREF="bizops.asp">Business Opportunities</A>
      <P><A HREF="communities.asp">Our Web Communities </A>
      <P><A HREF="mission.asp">Our Mission</A>
      <P><A HREF="us.asp">The People Under the Tent</A>
      <P><A HREF="feedback.asp">Contact Us</A>
      </DIV>
    </TD>
```

The navigational sidebar creates the need for a table. In a perfect world we would place this information into a list element like a UL and apply styles so that no bullet is used, and so that it floats to the left, however, browser support being what it is this simply wouldn't yield the results it should, so more conventional methods were used. At least styles can be mapped to the NAVIGATION class:

```
<TD BGCOLOR="#FFFFFF">
<P>Big Tent Media Labs is a publishing company that
creates printed and Web-based products, unique technology
tools, and innovative publishing strategies. We think
```

integrated print and Internet products are the future of
publishing, and we aim to build vibrant communities
around our interactive publishing projects. Our content-
rich sites target people with common interests who come
together online to discuss ideas and interact with the
content, which in turn builds an enduring community
around the publication.

<P>Big Tent Media Labs offers special know-how to
publishers because we're publishers ourselves. We help
publishers integrate their printed material with an
online presence, which gives their readers a richer
experience while giving the publisher enhanced business
opportunities.

<P>C'mon in and check out our exciting Web communities!

<A HREF="http://www.hipmama.com">

<IMG SRC="images/button_hipmama.gif" WIDTH=88 HEIGHT=31
BORDER=0></A>

<A HREF="http://www.internet-nexus.com">

<IMG SRC="images/button_nexus.gif" WIDTH=88 HEIGHT=31
BORDER=0></A>

<A HREF="http://www.lofy.com">

<IMG SRC="images/button_lofy.gif" WIDTH=88 HEIGHT=31
BORDER=0>

<DIV CLASS="LEGAL_STUFF">

Copyright ©1997 Big Tent Media Labs

</DIV>

<DIV CLASS="CONTACT">

<A HREF="mailto:thurrott@bigtent.com">

webmaster@bigtent.com

</A>

</DIV>

<DIV CLASS="MSIE">

Best experienced with

<A HREF="http://www.microsoft.com/ie/default.asp">

<IMG SRC="images/ie_animated.gif"

    ALT="Microsoft Internet Explorer"

    BORDER="0"

    VSPACE="3"

    WIDTH="88"

```
        HEIGHT="31">
<br>
Click here to start.
</A>
</TD></TR></TABLE>
```

We have added a couple of new classes here, including the **LEGAL_STUFF** for copyright notices and other small print, and the **CONTACT** class for contact information. Now the tables is closed, the page is finished, and it is time to create the style sheet.

The first order of business will be to define the presentation of the main header, in this case the "Welcome to Big Tent" text:

```
H1 { font-family: Ariel Sans-Serif;
     font-size: 3;
     font-width: bold;
     text-color: white;
     text-align: center;
     bgcolor: #663399;
     }
```

The second step is to assign some properties for the navigation sidebar:

```
DIV.NAVIGATION { font-family: ariel sans-serif;
                 font-size: 3;
                 }
```

Next, rules for the display of running text are assigned:

```
P.MAIN { font-family: ariel sans-serif;
         font-size: 3;
         text-align: justify;
         }
```

Finally, we handle the smaller items...

```
.LEGAL_STUFF { font-family: ariel sans-serif;
               font-size: 2;
               text-align: center;
               }
.CONTACT { font-family: courier monospace;
           font-size: 2;
           text-align: center;
           }
```

As you can see from Figure 13.2, the display of this new, simpler code is nearly identical to the original site!

Figure 13.2 The new CSS-based Big Tent site.

APPENDIX A

CSS Compatibility Chart

Web developers are always frustrated by the lack of compatibility between browsers and platforms. No two browsers act exactly the same way in all scenarios. Although CSS is supposed to combat this problem, in reality it often simply mirrors it with differing implementations of the spec.

To help you develop sites and know what to expect from different browsers Tables A.1 through A.5 describe browser support for each CSS feature.

Table A.1 Font Control

Feature	Internet Explorer 3 (Windows)	Internet Explorer 3 (MacOS)	Internet Explorer 4 (Windows)	Netscape 4 (Windows)	Netscape 4 (MacOS)
Font-family property	yes	yes	yes	yes	yes
Serif	yes	yes	yes	yes	yes
Sans-serif	yes	no	yes	yes	no
Cursive	yes	no	yes	no	no
Fantasy	yes	no	yes	no	no
Monospace	yes	yes	yes	yes	no

continued on next page

Table A.1 Font Control (continued)

Feature	Internet Explorer 3 (Windows)	Internet Explorer 3 (MacOS)	Internet Explorer 4 (Windows)	Netscape 4 (Windows)	Netscape 4 (MacOS)
Font-size property	yes	yes	yes	yes	partial
Absolute values	yes	yes	yes	yes	no
Length values	no	partial	no	partial	partial
Percentage values	partial	partial	yes	yes	no
XX-small	yes	yes	yes	no	no
X-small	yes	yes	yes	no	no
Small	yes	yes	yes	yes	no
Medium	yes	yes	yes	yes	no
Large	yes	yes	yes	yes	no
X-large	yes	yes	yes	yes	no
XX-large	yes	yes	yes	yes	no
Smaller	no	no	yes	yes	no
Larger	no	no	yes	yes	no
Font-style property	partial	partial	yes	yes	yes
Normal	no	no	yes	yes	yes
Italic	yes	yes	yes	yes	yes
Oblique	no	no	yes	yes	yes
Font-weight property	partial	partial	yes	partial	no
Bold	yes	yes	yes	yes	no
Extra-bold	yes	yes	yes	no	no
Bolder	no	no	yes	no	no
Lighter	no	no	yes	no	no
Numeric values (100–900)	no	no	partial	yes	partial
Font-variant property	no	no	yes	no	no
Small-caps	no	no	yes	no	no

Feature	Internet Explorer 3 (Windows)	Internet Explorer 3 (MacOS)	Internet Explorer 4 (Windows)	Netscape 4 (Windows)	Netscape 4 (MacOS)
Text-transform property	no	no	yes	yes	yes
Capitalize	no	no	yes	yes	yes
Uppercase	no	no	yes	yes	yes
Lowercase	no	no	yes	yes	yes
None	no	no	yes	yes	yes
Text-decoration property	partial	partial	partial	partial	partal
Underline	yes	yes	yes	yes	yes
Overline	no	no	yes	no	no
Line-through	yes	yes	yes	yes	yes
Blink	no	no	no	yes	yes
None	yes	yes	yes	yes	yes

Table A.2 Controlling Space

Feature	Internet Explorer 3 (Windows)	Internet Explorer 3 (MacOS)	Internet Explorer 4 (Windows)	Netscape 4 (Windows)	Netscape 4 (MacOS)
Word-spacing property	no	no	no	no	no
Letter-spacing property	no	no	yes	no	no
Line-height property	partial	partial	yes	yes	yes
Numerical value	partial	partial	yes	yes	yes

continued on next page

Table A.2 Controlling Space (continued)

Feature	Internet Explorer 3 (Windows)	Internet Explorer 3 (MacOS)	Internet Explorer 4 (Windows)	Netscape 4 (Windows)	Netscape 4 (MacOS)
Length value	yes	yes	yes	yes	yes
Percentage value	yes	yes	yes	yes	yes
Text-align property	partial	partial	yes	yes	yes
Left	yes	yes	yes	yes	yes
Center	yes	yes	yes	yes	yes
Right	yes	yes	yes	yes	yes
Justify	no	no	yes	yes	yes
Text-indent property	yes	yes	yes	yes	yes
Margin-top property	partial	yes	no	yes	yes
Length value	partial	yes	no	yes	yes
Percentage value	yes	yes	no	yes	yes
Auto	no	no	no	no	no
Margin-bottom property	partial	no	no	yes	yes
Length value	partial	no	no	yes	yes
Percentage value	partial	no	no	yes	yes
Auto	no	no	no	no	no
Margin-left property	yes	yes	yes	yes	yes
Length value	yes	yes	yes	yes	yes
Percentage value	yes	yes	yes	yes	yes
Auto	no	no	no	no	no
Margin-right property	yes	yes	partial	partial	partial
Length value	yes	yes	partial	partial	partial

Feature	Internet Explorer 3 (Windows)	Internet Explorer 3 (MacOS)	Internet Explorer 4 (Windows)	Netscape 4 (Windows)	Netscape 4 (MacOS)
Percentage value	yes	yes	partial	partial	partial
Auto	no	no	no	no	no
Margin property	partial	partial	partial	partial	partial
Length value	no	no	no	partial	partial
Percentage value	yes	yes	yes	partial	partial
Auto	no	no	no	no	no
Padding-top property	no	no	no	yes	yes
Length value	no	no	no	yes	yes
Percentage value	no	no	no	yes	yes
Padding-bottom property	no	no	no	yes	yes
Length value	no	no	no	yes	yes
Percentage value	no	no	no	yes	yes
Padding-left property	no	no	no	partial	partial
Length value	no	no	no	partial	partial
Percentage value	no	no	no	partial	partial
Padding-right property	no	no	no	partial	partial
Length value	no	no	no	partial	partial
Percentage value	no	no	no	partial	partial
Padding property	no	no	no	partial	partial
Length value	no	no	no	partial	partial

continued on next page

Table A.2 Controlling Space (continued)

Feature	Internet Explorer 3 (Windows)	Internet Explorer 3 (MacOS)	Internet Explorer 4 (Windows)	Netscape 4 (Windows)	Netscape 4 (MacOS)
Percentage value	no	no	no	partial	partial
Border control	no	no	partial	partial	partial
Width property	no	no	partial	yes	yes
Height property	no	no	partial	no	no
Float property	no	no	partial	yes	yes
Clear property	no	no	partial	yes	yes
Position property	no	no	partial	yes	yes
Absolute values	no	no	partial	yes	yes
Relative values	no	no	no	yes	yes
Visibility property	no	no	yes	partial	no
Inherit	no	no	yes	no	no
Visible	no	no	yes	no	no
Hidden	no	no	yes	yes	no
White-space property	no	no	partial	partial	partial
Normal	no	no	partial	yes	yes
Pre	no	no	partial	yes	yes
Nowrap	no	no	no	no	no

Table A.3 General CSS

Feature	Internet Explorer 3 (Windows)	Internet Explorer 3 (MacOS)	Internet Explorer 4 (Windows)	Netscape 4 (Windows)	Netscape 4 (MacOS)
Embedded Style Sheets	yes	yes	yes	yes	yes
Linked Style Sheets	yes	yes	yes	yes	yes

Feature	Internet Explorer 3 (Windows)	Internet Explorer 3 (MacOS)	Internet Explorer 4 (Windows)	Netscape 4 (Windows)	Netscape 4 (MacOS)
@import notation	no	no	no	no	no
Inline Styles (STYLE Attribute)	yes	yes	yes	yes	yes
A:link	yes	yes	yes	no	no
A:visited	no	partial	yes	no	no
A:active	no	no	yes	no	no
first-letter	no	no	no	no	no
first-line	no	no	no	no	no

Table A.4 Units of Measure

Feature	Internet Explorer 3 (Windows)	Internet Explorer 3 (MacOS)	Internet Explorer 4 (Windows)	Netscape 4 (Windows)	Netscape 4 (MacOS)
in (inch)	yes	yes	yes	yes	yes
cm (centimeter)	yes	yes	yes	yes	yes
mm (millimeter)	yes	yes	yes	yes	yes
pt (point)	yes	yes	yes	yes	yes
pc (pica)	yes	yes	yes	no	no
em	no	yes	no	partial	partial
ex (x-height)	no	yes	no	partial	partial
px (pixel)	yes	yes	yes	yes	yes
% (percentage)	yes	yes	yes	yes	yes

Table A.5 Colors in CSS

Feature	Internet Explorer 3 (Windows)	Internet Explorer 3 (MacOS)	Internet Explorer 4 (Windows)	Netscape 4 (Windows)	Netscape 4 (MacOS)
Named Colors	yes	yes	yes	yes	yes
Hex Values	yes	yes	yes	yes	yes
RGB Values	no	no	yes	yes	yes

For more information about colors, see Appendix B or the Web site at http://www.internet-nexus.com/css/color/.

Appendix B

CSS Reference

This appendix includes a table of named colors in HTML and CSS and a list of on-line resources for Web designers using CSS.

HTML/CSS Color Table

This list of colors includes all 256 of the named colors in HTML and CSS. For a full-color chart visit http://www.internet-nexus.com/css/colors/.

Aquamarine	70DB93
Baker's Chocolate	5C3317
Black	000000
Blue	0000FF
Blue Violet	9F4F9F
Brass	B5A642
Bright Gold	D9D919
Brown	A62A2A
Bronze II	A67D3D

Cadet Blue	5F9F9F
Cool Copper	D98719
Copper	B87333
Coral	FF7F00
Corn Flower Blue	42426F
Cyan	00FFFF
Dark Brown	5C4033
Dark Green	2F4F2F
Dark Green Copper	4A766E
Dark Olive Green	4F4F2F
Dark Orchid	9932CD
Dark Purple	871F78
Dark Slate Blue	6B238E
Dark Slate Gray	2F4F4F
Dark Tan	97694F
Dark Turquoise	7093DB
Dark Wood	855E42
Dim Gray	545454
Dusty Rose	856363
Feldspar	D19275
Firebrick	8E2323
Forest Green	238E23
Gold	CD7F32
Goldenrod	DBDB70
Gray ("Netscape Gray")	COCOCO
Green	00FF00
Green Copper	527F76
Green Yellow	93DB70
Hunter Green	215E21
Indian Red	4E2F2F
Khaki	9F9F5F
Light Blue	C0D9D9
Light Gray	A8A8A8
Light Steel Blue	8F8FBD
Light Wood	E9C2A6
Lime Green	32CD32

Magenta	FF00FF
Mandarin Orange	E47833
Maroon	8E236B
Medium Aquamarine	32CD99
Medium Blue	3232CD
Medium Forest Green	6B8E23
Medium Goldenrod	EAEAAE
Medium Orchid	9370DB
Medium Sea Green	426F42
Medium Slate Blue	7F00FF
Medium Spring Green	7FFF00
Medium Turquoise	70DBDB
Medium Violet Red	DB7093
Medium Wood	A68064
Midnight Blue	2F2F4F
Navy Blue	23238E
Neon Blue	4D4DFF
Neon Pink	DD6EC7
New Midnight Blue	00009C
New Tan	EBC79E
Old Gold	CFB53B
Orange	FF7F00
Orange Red	FF2400
Orchid	DB70DB
Pale Green	8FBC8F
Pink	BC8F8F
Plum	EAADEA
Quartz	D9D9F3
Red	FF0000
Rich Blue	5959AB
Salmon	6F4242
Scarlet	8C1717
Sea Green	238E68
Semi-Sweet Chocolate	6B4226
Sienna	8E6B23
Silver	E6E8FA

Sky Blue	3299CC
Slate Blue	007FFF
Spicy Pink	FF1CAE
Spring Green	00FF7F
Steel Blue	236B8E
Summer Sky	38B0DE
Tan	DB9370
Thistle	D8BFD8
Turquoise	ADEAEA
Very Dark Brown	5C4033
Very Light Gray	CDCDCD
Violet	4F2F4F
Violet Red	CC3299
Wheat	D8D8BF
White	FFFFFF
Yellow	FFFF00
Yellow Green	33CC32

ON-LINE RESOURCES

Internet Nexus	http://www.internet-nexus.com
The World Wide Web Consortium (W3C)	http://www.w3.org
Microsoft Typography Site	http://www.microsoft.com/typography/
Microsoft Site Builder Network	http://www.microsoft.com/sitebuilder
Microsoft Site Builder Workshop	http://www.microsoft.com/workshop
David Siegel's "Web Wonk"	http://www.dsiegel.com/tips/index.html
Style Sheets Resource Centre	http://peavine.com/CSS/ns/
Cascading Style Sheets Working Draft	http://www.w3.org/TR/REC-CSS1 961217
Netscape Communications	http://home.netscape.com

APPENDIX C

The Future of CSS

Coming soon to a browser near you—CSS2!

Sitting on the W3C committee must be a tough job—just as one specification is completed and accepted by the committee, new ones must be presented and considered. In this case, it is the successor to the CSS spec that is on the table.

The W3C committee is considering several innovations for the next version of the spec, some of the more promising proposals are included here.

 For the latest information, visit the Web site at http://www.internet-nexus.com/css/appendix/css2/.

TEXT SHADOWS

Although text shadows can be accomplished with workarounds in conventional CSS, the developers of the specification promise an easier way to create this effect: a text-shadow property.

Users will be able to control the offset, color, and possibly even the focus of the shadow using this property.

CURSOR CONTROL

Using Microsoft's Dynamic HTML, designers can control the user's cursor, and the next version of the CSS specification, dubbed CSS2, promises to offer the same control.

Basically, designers would be able to control what the cursor looks like when over each element using the cursor property. Allowed values should include, but not be limited to the following:

- auto
- crosshair
- default
- hand
- "wait" state
- "editable text" cursor (usually an I-Beam)

FILTERS AND TEXT EFFECTS

The W3C is currently working on methods for applying a rich set of special effects to text and images such as image blurring and glow effects. The purpose would be to enable the use of CSS for the modification of existing structural elements to be presented in new and innovative ways instead of creating bitmapped images to accomplish the same effect, impacting download time.

MULTICOLUMN LAYOUT

There are two draft specifications on the W3C's table for consideration for multicolumn layout. Because no firm decisions had been made at the time of this writing, no information is provided here. For the latest information, visit http://www.internet-nexus.com/css/appendix/css2/.

FONT DESCRIPTORS

The current CSS spec allows for the addition of various font properties to HTML elements. The problem is that fonts are assumed to be present on the client system and are identified solely by name (and one of five generic families).

CSS2 will build on and extend the CSS1 font model to allow font descriptions to be added to a style sheet. These font descriptions will consist of a set of font descriptors, individual pieces of information about a font, possibly including a URL where the font can be downloaded. This will provide additional capabilities:

- intelligent client-side selection of a suitable font from the collection of fonts known to the platform or user agent
- synthesis of a replacement font
- downloading a font provided over the Web

APPENDIX D

HTML Tables Reference

Introduced as one of Netscape's HTML extensions in Navigator 1.1, tables were immediately embraced by Web developers, and have been continually improved by Netscape, Microsoft, and even the W3C. Designers see tables as the cornerstone of advanced layout on the Web, since they are much more widely supported than more recent additions like Absolute Positioning or Netscape's `<LAYER>` tag.

There are two problems with complex table-based layouts:

1. Code can become cumbersome, complex, and difficult to manage.
2. With seriously complex designs taking advantage of tables nested several levels deep, some browsers will consume prodigious amounts of memory, and even crash. (This happened more often in older browsers, but is still an issue.)

GENERAL TABLE SYNTAX

The first tag you need to familiarize yourself with when dealing with tables is, surprisingly enough, the **<TABLE>** tag. This is a block-level tag, similar in concept to a **BODY** element, or a **BLOCKQUOTE**. The table is contained within the TABLE tags.

```
<TABLE>
Here is your table!
</TABLE>
```

Obviously, the example above isn't really a complete table, since no information about the structure of the table has been provided. This is done by using the **<TR>** (Table Row) and **<TD>** (Table Data) elements.

```
<TABLE>
  <TR>
    <TD>
      Here is some content
    </TD>
  </TR>
</TABLE>
```

The code above is essentially the most simple table possible in HTML: it has only one cell, and contains no additional information about how to display and format the table. However, it is enough information for the browser to display the table pictured in Figure D.1.

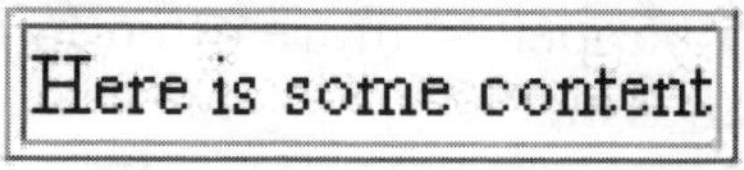

Figure D.1 A simple table as displayed in Explorer.

When looking at the code you notice the hierarchy of the elements: the **\<TR>** element is a child of the **\<TABLE>** element, and the **\<TD>** element is a child of the **\<TR>** element. It is important to understand these relationships when assigning additional values to each element in order to take advantage of inheritance.

Most tables won't be this simple.

PRODUCT	PRICE	QTY.
Sony Monitor, 21"	$1399.00	1
Pentium 200 CPU	$1200.00	1

Figure D.2 A slightly more complex table.

In the table pictured in Figure D.2 you can see a simple layout taking shape. Still, though, the format is that of a simple tabular layout.

```
<TABLE>
   <TR>
      <TD>
         PRODUCT
      </TD>
      <TD>
         PRICE
      </TD>
      <TD>
         QTY.
      </TD>
   </TR>
   <TR>
      <TD>
         Sony Monitor, 21"
```

```
  </TD>
  <TD>
    $1399.00
  </TD>
  <TD>
    1
  </TD>
  </TR>
 <TR>
  <TD>
    Pentium 200 CPU
  </TD>
  <TD>
    $1200.00
  </TD>
  <TD>
    1
  </TD>
  </TR>
 </TABLE>
```

Let's take a look at what is happening here:
The first thing that happens is the table is established.

```
<TABLE>
```

Then the first row of the table is established. This row will actually take the role of handling "header" information for the individual columns. There is actually a **<TH>** (Table Heading) element in the HTML tables specification, but it is of limited usefulness, since most browsers won't allow you to map styles to **TH** elements. In general, and in this example, **<TR>** elements are used.

Note the indentation, signifying that the **<TR>** element is a child of the **<TABLE>** element.

```
<TR>
```

Next, the first column in the first row is created, and content is placed inside it.

```
<TD>
    PRODUCT
</TD>
```

Some additional columns are created within this row, each essentially identical to the first except for the content.

```
<TD>
    PRICE
</TD>
<TD>
    QTY.
</TD>
```

And, of course, the **<TR>** element is closed off.

```
</TR>
```

Next, the second and third rows are created, and the **<TABLE>** element is closed off.

Now this table, although more complex then the first example, is still a very simplistic view of this powerful specification. Several attributes exist for each of the elements within a table.

THE BORDER ATTRIBUTE

The **BORDER** attribute is fairly self-explanatory: it controls table borders. Let's say, for instance, that you have designed a table that controls layout, but should remain invisible. You would need to turn borders off using the following code:

```
<TABLE BORDER="0">
```

The values are numeric, and represent pixel measurements. Therefore, a value of 6 would produce a 6 pixel wide border around the table.

THE ALIGN ATTRIBUTE

The **ALIGN** attribute can be applied to the table element or individual **<TR>** and **<TD>** elements within the table. When applied to a **<TR>** or **<TD>** element, the **ALIGN** attribute will control the alignment of content within that table cell or group of cells. There are three possible values: **RIGHT**, **LEFT**, and **CENTER**. While the ALIGN attribute is often applied to individual **<TD>** elements, it can also be applied to a **<TR>** element, and will be inherited by the child **<TD>** elements.

When applied to the **<TABLE>** element the **ALIGN** attribute behaves much like it would when applied to an image. A table with the **RIGHT** value applied to the **ALIGN** attribute would float to the right much like an image, with content wrapping around the table as displayed in Figure D.3.

Figure D.3 The ALIGN Attribute at work.

THE VALIGN ATTRIBUTE

The **VALIGN** attribute, much like the **ALIGN** attribute, is used to control the alignment of content within table cells. However, **VALIGN** controls the verticle alignment rather than the horizontal alignment. The available values are **TOP, BOTTOM,** and **MIDDLE.**

THE NOWRAP ATTRIBUTE

By default, content within tables is allowed to wrap when it runs out of space horizontally. However, sometimes this is not the desired effect. In these cases, you can apply the **NOWRAP** attribute to either the whole table or individual rows and cells to stop the content from wrapping.

COLSPAN AND ROWSPAN

You probably won't always want to create simple tabular structures with tables. Often, you will use them to create complex page layouts. The most important attributes when doing more complex designs are **COLSPAN** and **ROWSPAN**, which allow individual cells to span the width or height of several other cells.

COLSPAN

COLSPAN defines how many columns an element should span. For example:

```
<TR>
        <TD> Cell 1 </TD>
        <TD COLSPAN=2> Cell 2 </TD>
        <TD> Cell 3 </TD>
</TR>
```

In this example, the second cell is told to span two columns of height, and when placed into a table, can produce output like Figure D.4.

Figure D.4 **COLSPAN** *applied to a TD element.*

ROWSPAN

ROWSPAN is exactly like **COLSPAN**, except that it represents the amount of rows that should be spanned, rather than columns. Let's use a similar example:

```
<TR>
      <TD> Cell 1 </TD>
      <TD ROWSPAN=2> Cell 2 </TD>
      <TD> Cell 3 </TD>
</TR>
```

In this example, the second cell will span two rows like in Figure D.5.

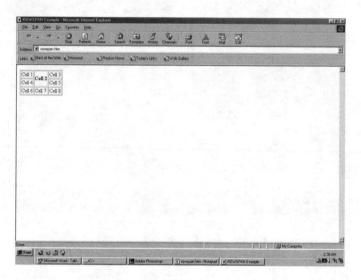

Figure D.5 ROWSPAN at work.

CELLSPACING AND CELLPADDING

CELLSPACING and **CELLPADDING** define the way space is handled in the table.

CELLSPACING

CELLSPACING controls the amount of space between the different cells in a table. This is important in designs that depend on precisely spaced elements.

You can see the difference a little space can make in Figure D.6.

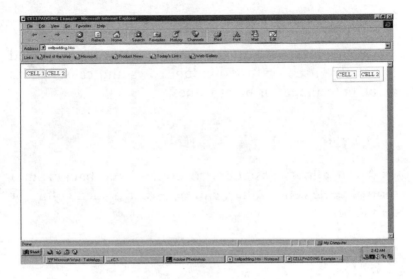

*Figure D.6 **CELLSPACING** in an HTML table.*

In this example, the window on the left has the following **TABLE** element:

```
<TABLE BORDER="1" CELLSPACING="2">
```

while the window on the right has this:

```
<TABLE BORDER="1" CELLSPACING="10">
```

CELLPADDING

CELLPADDING is the amount of space between the border of the cell and the contents of the cell. This is important in designs that control background color of cells using the **BGCOLOR** attribute, and in designs that use borders on tables.

HEIGHT AND WIDTH

HEIGHT and **WIDTH** are fairly simple, and can be applied to the table itself or to individual rows and cells. Values can be percentages or pixel values.

BGCOLOR AND BACKGROUND

BGCOLOR allows designers to control the background color of table cells. Values can be either named colors or RGB values.

Table Colors first appeared in Internet Explorer 2.0, but were not supported by Netscape until version 3.0. When using table colors make sure to test your designs in Netscape 2.0!

The **BACKGROUND** element allows you to define a repeating pattern graphic for the background of a table cell instead of a solid color. This feature is not yet widely supported, though, so make sure if you use it you define a **BGCOLOR** as well so that things will display reasonably well in unsupported browsers. Values to the **BACKGROUND** attribute should be image files, usually .gif or .jpg files.

GETTING MORE INFORMATION

The tables specification is constantly evolving for the latest information, visit the Web site at http://www.internet-nexus.com/web/cssbook/tables.asp.

APPENDIX E

Frames

Frames are used to better organize information on a Web site. Used correctly, frames provide a valuable navigational aid to otherwise complex sites. Used recklessly, like the aberration shown in Figure E.1, frames make it hard for the user to navigate around a site.

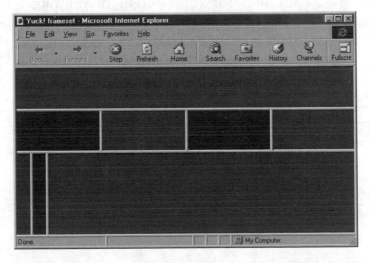

Figure E.1 A carelessly designed frameset is ugly and hard to use.

This appendix consists of two main sections: a short frames tutorial and a frames reference you can refer to as you create frames-based sites.

FRAMES TUTORIAL

To create your own frames-based sites, you need to understand some basic frames terminology. Whenever you see a frames-based site, there is an underlying frameset that determines the layout of the frames used by the site. The frameset is like a container for frames. Each frame in the frameset contains an HTML page. With that in mind, let's take a look at some simple framesets.

USING FRAMESETS AND FRAMES

When you develop a non-frames page, the **BODY** section acts as a container for the content in the page. For frames-based pages, the FRAMESET section, demarked by **<FRAMESET>** and **</FRAMESET>** tags, replaces the familiar **BODY** section. Consider the following HTML file:

```
<HTML>
<HEAD><TITLE>Simple frameset</TITLE></HEAD>
<FRAMESET COLS="25%, 75%">
      <FRAME SRC="red.html" NAME="nav">
      <FRAME SRC="blue.html" NAME="main">
</FRAMESET>
</HTML>
```

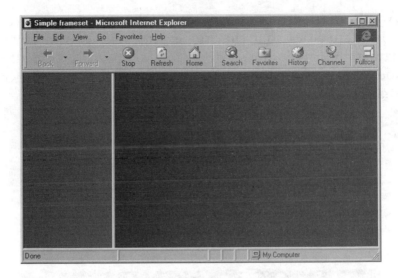

Figure E.2 *When you specify a frameset with the COLS attribute, the frames appear in a vertical layout.*

The output from this code is shown in Figure E.2. As you can see, the frameset consists of two frames. The layout is vertical, with the frames occupying two columns. This is due to the **COLS** attribute in the **FRAMESET** tag. The **COLS** attribute specifies a vertical layout and lets you determine the size of each frame. In this case, the leftmost frame will occupy 25% of the width of the browser and the rightmost frame will occupy the other 75%. You can specify as many columns as you'd like, as well. If you wanted to use three columns, for example, with widths of 100 pixels, 50 pixels, and a third column taking up the remainder of the width, you might use code like this:

```
<FRAMESET COLS="100, 50, *">
```

An alternative to **COLS** is to use the **ROWS** attribute, which specifies that the frames are arranged in rows rather than columns. The following code is virtually identical to the previous example, but uses rows rather than columns.

```
<HTML>
<HEAD><TITLE>Simple frameset</TITLE></HEAD>
<FRAMESET ROWS="25%, 75%">
        <FRAME SRC="red.html" NAME="nav">
        <FRAME SRC="blue.html" NAME="main">
</FRAMESET>
</HTML>
```

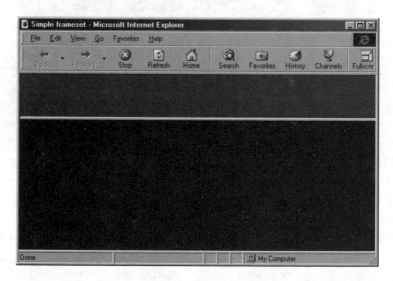

Figure E.3 When you specify a frameset with the ROWS attribute, the frames appear in a horizontal layout.

As shown in Figure E.3, this file creates a horizontally-arranged frameset, with a small frame on the top and a larger frame on the bottom.

Targeting Frames

The primary reason to use frames is to simplify navigation. Generally, a good frames-based site will have two frames, a small frame featuring a navigational button bar or menu, and the larger main frame. The previous two examples, one horizontal and one vertical, shows this sort of layout. You might have noticed the **NAME** attribute used in both of the **FRAME** tags. This specifies a name for the frame so you can target it in a hyperlink. For example, if you want to target the frame named *main* from the navigational frame, you might use code such as the following:

```
<P><A HREF="http://www.microsoft.com"
TARGET="main">Microsoft</A>
```

Then, when the hyperlink is clicked, the specified page will load in the correct frame. This is shown in Figure E.4.

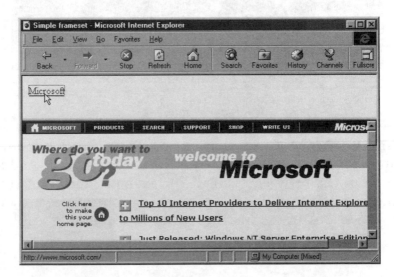

Figure E.4 It's easy to target frames with HTML.

Specifying a Border

By default, a frameset will display a 3D border between each of its frames. If you'd like to remove this border, you can use the **FRAMEBORDER** attribute. **FRAMEBORDER** can be set to 0 or 1. If 0 is used, no border will be drawn, as shown in Figure E.5. If you set it to 1, the normal 3D border is drawn.

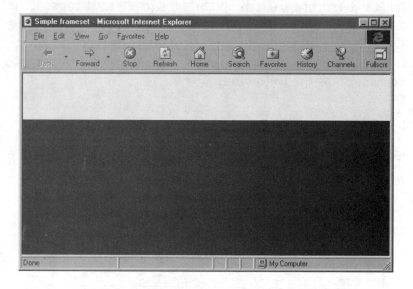

Figure E.5 A frameset with no 3D border.

The **FRAMESET** tag also supports another border attribute called **FRAMESPACING** that allows you to add white space between frames. For example, the frameset shown in Figure E.6 has a 5 pixel space between its two frames. This was done by setting **FRAMEBORDER** to 0 and **FRAMESPACING** to 5.

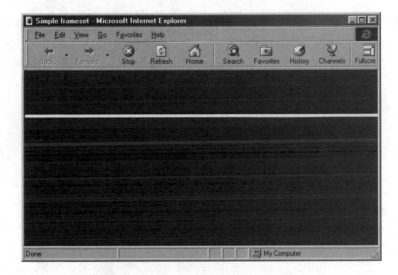

Figure E.6 You can easily add space between frames with the
FRAMESPACING *attribute.*

USING FLOATING FRAMES

Internet Explorer 3.0 introduced the floating frame, a
new type of frame that floats independently somewhere
in the middle of the browser. Floating frames are created
with the **IFRAME** tag, but since thye are only supported
in Internet Explorer 3.0 and up, we won't spend much
time on them here. The reference section below contains
a section on **IFRAME**, however.

HANDLING OLDER BROWSERS

Frames are nice if the user's browser supports them, but
if not you'll need some way to get content to those users.
This is done with a **NOFRAMES** block that you place

below the **FRAMESET** block. For example, the following code displays a frameset if the user's browser supports frames. Otherwise, a message is displayed asking the user to upgrade.

```
<HTML>
<HEAD><TITLE>Paul's menu</TITLE></HEAD>
<FRAMESET ROWS="50, *">
       <FRAME SRC="nav.html" NAME="nav">
       <FRAME SRC="main.html" NAME="main">
</FRAMESET>
<NOFRAMES>
<B>Sorry, this site requires a frames-capable
browser.</B>
</NOFRAMES>
</HTML>
```

If you're adventurous and don't mind supporting two versions of your site, you can actually use the **NOFRAMES** block just like a **BODY** block in a normal HTML page and provide a no-frames version of each page. This is laborious at best, however, and by this point most people browsing the Web have a frames-capable browser.

FRAMES REFERENCE

FRAMESET

```
<FRAMESET
COLS="[column widths]"
FRAMEBORDER="[1 or 0]"
FRAMESPACING="[spacing value]"
ROWS="[row heights]">
</FRAMESET>
```

COLS=[column widths]

When you use this tag, your frameset uses columns, not rows. You cannot use the **ROWS** attribute with **COLS**, only one of the two is allowed. The column widths can be specified as exact pixel amounts, percentages (%), or relative size (*).

Examples:

COLS="100,*"   Creates a vertical frameset with one 100 pixel column. The other column occupies the remainder of the browser width.

COLS="50%, 50%"   Creates a vertical frameset with two equal-width frames, regardless of the browser width.

FRAMEBORDER=[1 or 0]

The **FRAMEBORDER** attribute determines whether the frameset uses a 3D border. It can be set to 1 (to use the border) or 0 (no border).

FRAMESPACING=[spacing value]

FRAMESPACING can be used to create additional space between frames in a frameset. It can be set to 0 or any positive numerical value. To create a space of 5 pixels between frames, set **FRAMESPACING** to 5.

ROWS=[row heights]

When you use this tag, your frameset uses rows, not columns. You cannot use the **ROWS** and **COLS** attributes together in the same frameset, only one of the two is allowed. The row heights can be specified as exact pixel amounts, percentages (%), or relative size (*).

Examples:

ROWS="100,*"   Creates a horizontal frameset with one 100 pixel row. The other row occupies the remainder of the browser height.

ROWS="25%, 25%,50%"   Creates a horizontal frameset with three rows. The top two rows both occupy 25% of the browser height, the final row occupies 50%.

FRAME

```
<FRAME
FRAMEBORDER=" [1 or 0] "
MARGINHEIGHT=" [height in pixels] "
MARGINWIDTH=" [width in pixels] "
NAME=" [frame name] "
SCROLLING=" [YES or NO] "
SRC=" [address] ">
```

FRAMEBORDER="[1 or 0]"

Determines whether a 3D border is drawn around the frame. If set to 1, a 3D border is drawn. A value of 0 indicates no border.

MARGINHEIGHT="[height in pixels]"

Determines the margin height of the frame, in pixels. **MARGINHEIGHT** can be 0 or any positive integer value.

A value of 5, for example, would set the margin height to 5 pixels.

MARGINWIDTH="[width in pixels]"

Determines the margin width of the frame, in pixels. **MARGINWIDTH** can be 0 or any positive integer value. A value of 2, for example, would set the margin width to 2 pixels.

NAME="[frame name]"

The **NAME** attribute allows you to name the frame so that it can be targeted by hyperlinks or scripting code. The name can be any valid string, such as "MyFrame" or "Nav_Frame".

SCROLLING="[YES or NO]"

Determines whether the frame can scroll should the content in that frame take up a greater amount of space then the frame provides. When set to **"YES"**, scrollbars will appear if necessary. If set to **"NO"**, no scroll bars will appear.

SRC="[address]"

Determines the HTML file that will occupy the frame. For example, if you wished to display the file help.html in a frame named **HelpFrame**, you could use the following code:

```
<FRAME NAME="HelpFrame" SRC="help.html">
```

IFRAME

```
<FRAME
ALIGN=" [LEFT|CENTER|RIGHT|TOP|BOTTOM] "
FRAMEBORDER="[1 or 0]"
```

```
HEIGHT="[height in pixels]"
MARGINHEIGHT="[height in pixels]"
MARGINWIDTH="[width in pixels]"
NAME="[frame name]"
SCROLLING="[YES or NO]"
SRC="[address]"
WIDTH="[width in pixels]">
</IFRAME>
```

ALIGN="[LEFT|CENTER|RIGHT|TOP|BOTTOM]"

The **ALIGN** attribute determines the alignment of the floating frame or of text surrounding the floating frame. Possible values:

LEFT   The frame is drawn as a left-flush floating frame, causing text to flow around it.

CENTER   Surrounding text aligns with the center of the text.

RIGHT   The frame is drawn as a right-flush floating frame, causing text to flow around it.

TOP   Surrounding text aligns with the top of the floating frame.

BOTTOM   Surrounding text aligns with the bottom of the floating frame.

FRAMEBORDER="[1 or 0]"

Determines whether a 3D border is drawn around the floating frame. If set to 1, a 3-D border is drawn. A value of 0 indicates no border.

HEIGHT="[height in pixels]"

Determines the height of the floating frame, in pixels. **HEIGHT** can be 0 or any positive integer value. A value of 200, for example, would set the height to 200 pixels.

MARGINHEIGHT="[height in pixels]"

Determines the margin height of the floating frame, in pixels. **MARGINHEIGHT** can be 0 or any positive integer value. A value of 5, for example, would set the margin height to 5 pixels.

MARGINWIDTH="[width in pixels]"

Determines the margin width of the floating frame, in pixels. **MARGINWIDTH** can be 0 or any positive integer value. A value of 2, for example, would set the margin width to 2 pixels.

NAME="[frame name]"

The **NAME** attribute allows you to name the floating frame so that it can be targeted by hyperlinks or scripting code. The name can be any valid string, such as **"MyFloatingFrame"** or **"Nav_Frame"**.

SCROLLING="[YES or NO]"

Determines whether the floating frame can scroll should the content in that frame take up a greater amount of space then the frame provides. When set to **"YES"**, scrollbars will appear if necessary. If set to **"NO"**, no scroll bars will appear.

SRC="[address]"

Determines the HTML file that will occupy the floating frame. For example, if you wished to display the file tip.html in a floating frame named **"FFrame"**, you could use the following code:

```
<IFRAME NAME="FFrame" WIDTH="100" HEIGHT="100"
SCROLLING="YES"
  SRC="tip.htm"></IFRAME>
```

WIDTH="[width in pixels]"

Determines the width of the floating frame, in pixels. **WIDTH** can be any positive integer value. A value of 150, for example, would set the width to 150 pixels.

NOFRAMES

```
<NOFRAMES><!— Content for older browsers —></NOFRAMES>
```

The **NOFRAMES** tag is used to provide content to users with older browsers that do not support frames.
    Example:

```
<NOFRAMES>
```

You must use a frames-capable browser to view this site!

```
</NOFRAMES>
```

APPENDIX F

HTML Reference for CSS

This book assumes you have a basic knowledge of HTML. If you need a refresher course, you can refer to the Web sitefor this book (http://internet-nexus/web/design.asp), where several great tutorials are referenced. However, even those to whom HTML tags and structures are old hat sometimes need a quick reference. This appendix won't attempt to cover every facet of the extended HTML 3.2 spec, but rather the more structural tags you are most likely to come across in CSS-based documents.

STANDARD HTML TAGS

ANCHORS

Anchors are among the most important HTML tags, since they are the basis for linking in hypertext documents. The code

```
You can <A HREF="somefile.htm">
click here </A> to go somewhere else.
```

will take the user to the referenced file location when they click on the text between the HTML tags. Hyperlinked text is usually displayed in a different color from the rest of the running text, and it is often underlined.

Hyperlinks are actually one of the pseudo elements in CSS because they can be assigned different rules based on their state: regular links, visited links, and active links. For example:

```
A.visited { color: purple }
A.active { color: red }
A.link { color: blue;
         font-weight: bold; }
```

would make links blue, visited links purple, and active links red.

Anchors can also reference a specific place in a page using the NAME property.

If, for instance, you place the tag **<A NAME="top">** at the top of the document, and then create a link lower in the page to **<A HREF="#top">** clicking on the link will return the user to the top of the page. These anchors can be placed anywhere in the document, and will not have any effect on display.

THE BLOCKQUOTE TAG

The **BLOCKQUOTE** tag was intended to provide a construct for marking quotations within running text. Usually, this is displayed by indenting both the left and right margins of the text enclosed within the tags.

```
<BLOCKQUOTE>
An intellectual snob is someone who can listen to the
William Tell Overture and not think of the Lone Ranger
&mdash; Dan Rather
</BLOCKQUOTE>
```

The **BLOCKQUOTE** tag can, however, be used to set apart any block of text that should remain separate from the rest of the text. Using CSS, you can map a variety of styles to **BLOCKQUOTE** sections, so you can use this tag for sidebars and other bits and pieces of text.

DIV AND SPAN

DIV and **SPAN** were introduced specifically for CSS. They provide a construct through which users can mark up areas that should have styles applied to them without having any effect on non-CSS browsers This means that many things that would have been handled with proprietary tags can now be handled with nothing more than a simple style sheet and a couple of **DIV** and **SPAN** tags. The difference between the two is that **DIV** is a block level tag, while **SPAN** is inline.

```
<P>The SPAN tag provides a way to set text <SPAN>within a
block</SPAN> apart so the designer can map styles to that
segment of text.
<DIV> The DIV tag provides a way to set entire blocks of
text apart for style sheets. </DIV>
```

HEADINGS

Headings, such as **H1**, provide a construct for the management of various levels of headings within a document. HTML provides 6 levels: **H1**, **H2**, **H3**, **H4**, **H5**, and **H6**.

Headings are traditionally rendered in boldface text, and higher-level headings are usually displayed in larger text:

```
<H1> A Level One Heading </H1>
<H2> A Level Two Heading </H2>
```

EM AND STRONG

Although most designers have grown used to using the `<I>` and `<B>` tags, the functionally similar structural tags `<EM>` and `<STRONG>` provide the same effects and are more appropriate for use in CSS.

```
The <EM> EM tag </EM> stands for "emphasis," and is
usually rendered in italic type.
The <STRONG> STRONG tag </STRONG> is usually rendered in
boldface type.
```

`<EM>` and `<STRONG>` are supported by all browsers, and because they are more structural, lend themselves better to changing their display. For example, say you want to emphasize text by creating a "hi-liter" effect. You could do so by using the following CSS rule:

```
EM { background: yellow;
     font-style: normal;}
```

As you can see, this makes more sense than using `<I>` because the text isn't intended to be italicized.

OL, UL, AND LI

`OL` and `UL` provide constructs for structured lists in HTML. `OL`, or ordered list, creates a numbered list, and `UL`, or unordered list, creates a bulleted list.

CSS was designed with several constructs for managing lists, but unfortunately little if any of this portion of the spec is supported by the browser developers.

For instance, the list-style property in CSS is supposed to allow designers to change the way lists are displayed, but neither Internet Explorer nor Netscape fully supports this feature.

A list is created as a block element, and each list item is marked with a **<LI>** element, which will be replaced by the HTML parsing engine with a bullet. The type of bullet is defined by the type and level of the list. **<LI>**, or list item, doesn't need to be closed off with a **</LI>** tag.

```
<OL>
   <LI> List Item 1
   <LI> List Item 2
   <LI> List Item 3
</OL>
```

COMMONLY USED SPECIAL CHARACTERS

Symbol	Code
©	&copy;
®	&reg;
™	&trade;
—	&mdash;
&	&amp;
>	&gt;
<	&lt;
(Nonbreaking Space)	

Index

N

O

X